W9-CAZ-473

The Anti-Abortion Movement
and the Rise of the Religious Right

From Polite to Fiery Protest

SOCIAL MOVEMENTS PAST AND PRESENT

Irwin T. Sanders, Editor

The Anti-Abortion Movement and the Rise of the Religious Right

From Polite to Fiery Protest

Dallas A. Blanchard

Twayne Publishers • New York
Maxwell Macmillan Canada • Toronto
Maxwell Macmillan International • New York Oxford Singapore Sydney

The Anti-Abortion Movement and the Rise of the Religious Right: From Polite to Fiery Protest
Dallas A. Blanchard

Copyright © 1994 by Twayne Publishers
All rights reserved. No part of this book may be reproduced or transmitted in any form or by any means, electronic or mechanical, including photocopying, recording, or by any information storage and retrieval system, without permission in writing from the Publisher.

Twayne Publishers
Macmillan Publishing Company
866 Third Avenue
New York, New York 10022

Maxwell Macmillan Canada, Inc.
1200 Eglinton Avenue East
Suite 200
Don Mills, Ontario M3C 3N1

Library of Congress Cataloging-in-Publication Data

Blanchard, Dallas A.
 The anti-abortion movement and the rise of the religious right: from polite to fiery protest/Dallas A. Blanchard.
  p.   cm.—(Social movements past and present)
 Includes bibliographical references and index.
 ISBN 0-8057-3872-X.—ISBN 0-8057-3871-1 (pbk.)
 1. Pro-life movement—United States—History. 2. Abortion—United States—History. I. Title. II. Series.
HQ767.5.U5B58   1994   93-38457
363.4'6'0973—dc20   CIP

The paper used in this publication meets the minimum requirements of American National Standard for Information Sciences—Permanence of Paper for Printed Library Materials. ANSI Z3948-1984. ∞™

10 9 8 7 6 5 4 3 2 1 (hc)
10 9 8 7 6 5 4 3 2 1 (pbk)

Printed in the United States of America

For Glenda

If you are witness to anything that needs to be set straight, then you must tell about it.
—JOHN WEITZ, QUOTED IN READER'S DIGEST, FEBRUARY 1993

Contents

Acknowledgments

No book is the sole responsibility of a single author. This one would not have been possible without the assistance and information furnished by innumerable others.

Important resources and leads were provided by Lisa Swanson of the Washington, D.C., office of the National Abortion Rights Action League; Ann Baker of the National Center for the Pro-Choice Majority; Jane Harvey of the General Board of Church and Society of the United Methodist Church; Anne L. Sollee and Gina Shaw of the National Abortion Federation; Patricia Baird Windle of the Aware Woman Clinic; Greg Phares, chief of Baton Rouge Police Department; Chip Sams; Steve Baker of the Bureau of Alcohol, Tobacco, and Firearms; Mike Salick; Matt Friedman of the People for the American Way; and Michael Reynolds. Undoubtedly, there are a number of others whom I have unintentionally overlooked.

I cannot say enough about the contribution of Carol Chin, my Twayne editor. Throughout the preparation of the manuscript she continually astounded me with the breadth of her knowledge and her ability to pose insightful and penetrating questions and criticisms. Between Carol and Irwin Sanders, general editor for the social movements series, this work is far better than it might otherwise have been.

At this point an author is expected to assume sole responsibility for the work and absolve all those who helped. I would prefer to condemn (since I do not believe in hell, my condemnation has little effect other than symbolic, I realize) all those who refused to answer or return my calls and letters. I promise to ignore their critiques of this work.

Chapter 1

Framing the Discussion

The main text of this volume is devoted to the development and the dynamics of the anti-abortion movement in the United States. It attempts to answer the questions of how and why the movement arose and what its philosophies and inner workings consist of today. Before entering into that discusssion I would like to take a step back to frame it: to explain my use of terms—especially the term *anti-abortion*—and my application of social movement theory in general to the anti-abortion movement in particular.

A Note on Terminology

The terms *pro-life* and *pro-choice* are political statements by particular sides in the abortion controversy, and each side resents and protests the name(s) chosen by the other side.[1] Each wants to seize the high ground of the ethical/moral debate while appealing to as wide a constituency as possible. Those calling themselves pro-lifers hold that pro-choicers are really pro-death, while pro-choicers maintain that the pro-lifers are anti-woman.

Pro-life is in my view a misnomer; this position might be more accurately termed *pro-fetal-life* or *anti-abortion*. Some segments of the anti-abortion movement are closer to a broad pro-life stance, opposing not only abortion but also the death penalty, euthanasia, and the construction and deployment of nuclear, biological, and chemical weapons. But other groups not affiliated with the movement—approving abortion—

also oppose the death penalty and/or nuclear, biological, and chemical weapons. Sociologist Donald Granberg, in his 1982 essay "What Does It Mean to be 'Pro-Life'"? defines the pro-life position as one promoting gun control; opposing militarism and violence in the media; advocating high fertility (having a lot of children), medical research, and preventive medicine; opposing euthanasia, infanticide, suicide, and abortion; promoting exercise, blood donation, vegetarianism, highway safety (as opposed to drunk driving and speeding), conservation, and redistributive domestic and foreign aid policies; and opposing capital punishment (562–64). "Labeling oneself as 'pro-life,'" he asserts, "is a form of self-aggrandizement, in part because it casts aspersions on one's adversaries, implying that these opponents are 'anti-life'" (564). A similar position is held by James Kelly, a Catholic sociologist at Fordam University (1991).[2]

But the anti-abortion movement at large tends to ignore these issues, while some segments of the movement support the death penalty and the arms race. Moreover, many in the movement discount considerations of the implications of an unwanted pregnancy on the potential mother's life. Carol Maxwell (1991) suggests that individuals who join the movement are motivated less by its rhetoric employed than by their own life histories, circumstances, and values; that is, ethical principles are secondary. One might argue that the choice is not pure. In the extreme position, the choice for the fetus may be against the life of the woman, as in an ectopic pregnancy or the pregnancy of a pre-teenager. This argument could be extended in some cases of euthanasia and of nuclear, chemical, and biological warfare to ask, "Whose life is being given value over other lives?" As the conservative theologian Dietrich Bonhoeffer (1966) stated, "Life conflicts with life."

Thus, there are no purely neutral terms on which both sides, or even the public at large, can agree. I will use the terms *anti-abortion* and *pro-choice,* which appear to be in the widest use and which were adopted by the *Los Angeles Times* in 1982 and the *New York Times* in 1989.[3]

A Note on Social Movement Theory

A useful definition of *social movement*—what distinguishes it from other forms of collective behavior—comes from Anthony Blasi (1989:52): "social movements characteristically involve (1) opinions or beliefs which favor some kind of social change, (2) actions which further a change process, (3) intentions that the actions promote the change in question, (4) connectedness among the preferences and actions of a number of people, and (5) non-elite participation." As we shall see in the following pages, those involved in attempts to reverse or modify the U.S. Supreme Court 1973 rulings in *Roe v. Wade* and *Doe v. Bolton*, which gave broad support to a woman's right to have an abortion, clearly fit collectively into Blasi's definition. It is important to bear in mind that a *movement* is different from an *organization*. A social movement is usually composed of a number of organizations as well as of individuals acting outside those organizations. Furthermore, those organizations and individuals generally differ among themselves about the ultimate goals of the movement and the strategies and tactics to be used in achieving those various goals. There may be as much or more dispute and acrimony *within* a social movement as there is between it and the opposition.

There are also a number of disputes among those who observe social movements from some distance, the social theorists. Do social movements arise from spontaneous actions and emotions? Or are they the result of almost cold, calculating, rational planning? What is the importance of leadership styles and types in social movement success or expansion? Is there a better chance of success if the leaders are professionals or untrained part-timers? What fosters social movement development? What impedes it? Does violence, for example, help or hinder a movement in achieving its goals? What kinds of resources do movements need to persist or succeed? How important is rhetoric in the success or failure of a movement? What motivates people to involve themselves in a "moral crusade," such as prohibition, anti-pornography campaigns, and the anti-abortion movement? What constitutes movement "success?" How does the interaction between a movement and its opposition affect its development?

Michael Useem, in *Protest Movements in America* (1975), summarizes various explanations for the rise of social movements and characterizes three basic theories—structural functionalist, socio-psychological, and political-economic—that explain their reason for being. The following discussion of these theories will help us address some of the above questions with regard to the anti-abortion movement.

Structural-functionalism maintains that all systems—individuals, organizations, societies, and cultures—seek equilibrium, a steady, "comfortable" state. Changes in technology, for example, may lead to changes in the kinds of relationships in which people find themselves. In such a situation, traditional values cannot make sense of the changes, and a disjuncture arises between values and behavior, which is known as cognitive dissonance (Festinger 1957). William F. Ogburn (1964) defined this outcome of technological change as cultural lag, the tendency of values to slowly respond to technological and relationship change. Structural functionalism asserts that social movements rise out of such societal "strains" or disjunctures. It assumes that social systems as well as individuals seek stability and predictability. Social changes introduce disequilibrium, resulting in efforts to come to a new stable position.

The revitalization theory of anthropologist Anthony Wallace is a good example of structural functionalism. Wallace studied the Cargo Cults of the South Pacific that arose following World War II. Island natives had seen invasions first by the Japanese and then by the Americans. Especially in the latter case, the invasions were followed by huge imports of materials and supplies. Then, just as suddenly as they came, the invaders left, along with all their riches. The Cargo Cults arose in an attempt to explain, deal with, and resolve the resulting conflicts between traditional values and those arising with the sudden infusion and then loss of riches. On island after island there arose "prophets" predicting the imminent return of ships and planes with renewed materials. Wallace concluded that the Cargo Cults represented an attempt to mesh new experiences with traditional values and to reach a new social equilibrium.

In this light the anti-abortion movement, which arose following the liberalization of abortion laws in the 1960s and 1970s, could be viewed as an attempt to return to the status quo. Moreover, the seeming acceptance of abortion in society at large may be seen by movement participants as a highly charged symbol of a complex of social changes, such as the increased acceptability of single motherhood and sexual promiscuity and a devaluation of children. The movement, then, would be seeking to return to and reaffirm "traditional" values, those values in place prior to the social upheaval of the 1960s and 1970s. The problem with this analogy is that it is incomplete: Cargo Cults sought a new equilibrium that would incorporate the changes that had occurred; the anti-abortion movement appears to want to nullify change.

Another, and useful, example of structural functionalism is Neil J. Smelser's (1962) value-added approach. He maintains that social movements are either norm or value oriented. Norm-oriented movements center on instituting specific norms in society, while value-oriented movements seek to alter fundamentally the basic social structure. The anti-abortion movement has organizations that are both value and norm oriented. This mixture adds to its complexity and implies a tenuousness among the various coalitions within it.

Two basic views of behavior underlie *sociopsychological theory*. *Relative deprivation theory* asserts that when people perceive they are being unjustly deprived in relation to others they may form a movement to redress the wrongs. *Authoritarian personality theory* holds that authoritarians organize to impose their wills on others. Blanchard and Prewitt (1993) maintain that a desire to control the behavior of others underlies the anti-abortion movement. The original authoritarianism research (Adorno *et al.* 1952) arose from attempts to understand the acceptance of the actions of Hitler by most Germans. The researchers concluded that such acceptance was rooted in a cultural stress on obedience and submission to authority, usually in the form of a charismatic leader. The parallels to fundamentalism are clear. (See, for example, Shils, in Christie and Jahoda 1954; Photiadis and Johnson 1963; Kirscht and Dillehay 1967). Other studies have demonstrated a correlation between authoritarianism and the family ideology of the ideal fundamentalist family. For example, Levinson and Huffman (1955) found that authoritarianism correlates with an ideology of the autocratic family, which emphasizes conventionalism, authoritarian submission of women and children, exaggerated masculinity and femininity, and discipline. Furthermore, Frenkel-Brunswick (1954) found that authoritarian children, who usually come from authoritarian families, "tend to display authoritarian aggression, rigidity, cruelty, superstition, externalization and projectivity, denial of weakness, [and] power orientation; they also "more often hold dichotomous conceptions of sex roles, of kinds of people, and of values" (237).

Some researchers have concluded that the anti-abortion movement is an expression of relative deprivation. For example, Blanchard and Prewitt (1993) maintain that relative deprivation may have been a primary motivation behind the arsons and bombings of clinics and physicians' offices in the 1984–85 period.[4] As will be discussed in detail later in this volume, frustration with the lack of any real movement by the first Reagan administration may have led to more dramatic attempts to stop abortion, especially for those bombers and arsonists who had previously picketed and seen little, if any, change in the frequency of abortions. Other recent research concludes that this is not the case for the movement as a whole. Those involved in the larger movement apparently do not suffer from a personal loss of status but are concerned about the change in cultural values; that is, they operate out of a cultural fundamentalist position, which we will examine shortly. Blanchard and Prewitt (1993) conclude that those involved in violent activities are particularly motivated by the authoritarian personality syndrome. As we shall later see, however, this may explain the actions of only some segments of the movement.

Political-economic theory is based on four primary views of organizational behavior: (1) *authority conflict theory* asserts that movements form around the question of who is in charge of the course of social events (for example, many in the anti-abortion movement assert that there is a humanist conspiracy to replace the Judeo-Christian heritage, which they maintain was the founding tradition of the United States); (2) *mass-elite links theory* contends that intermediate organizations form to provide the mass with access to the elite, leading to protest bases in mass associations; (3) *resource mobilization theory* concentrates on the organizations within social movements and their abilities to garner essential resources (this approach has largely ignored the reasons why movements arise in the first place and the role(s) of values in both the rise and maintenance of movements); (4) *conflict, or Marxist, theory* suggests that movements arise from the contradictions inherent in capitalist societies, particularly from conflicts between social classes (the abortion conflict could thus be viewed as a battle between the working class, which tends to value larger families, and the middle and upper classes, which tend to value smaller families; the anti-abortion movement, however, spans all social classes, and social class appears to affect more the form of movement participation than participation itself).

There is some support for the authority conflict position in examining the anti-abortion movement. This position has some correlations with the authoritarian personality position. Blanchard and Prewitt (1993), for example, hold that the extreme elements of the movement, particularly religious fundamentalists, want to return to a kind of medieval culture in which religion dominates all other social institutions: family, politics, education, and economics. This is particularly, but not solely, true of Christian Reconstructionists, who would institute Old Testament law as the basis of the legal system and would allow only committed Christians to be judges, to teach, and to hold public office. (See Moyers 1991.)

The mass-elite links theory might conclude that the anti-abortion movement arose primarily from a disaffected group, perhaps working-class religious fundamentalists, who lack access to the political system. This would lead to alienation and protest activities to get the attention of those in power. To an extent, this might offer insights into the movement, particularly prior to 1980. The rise of the Moral Majority and the New Right, for example, appears to have come from those feeling they were not equitably represented in government. Fundamentalist charges of dominance by secular humanists give credence to this position. These same groups, however, took credit for the elections of Jimmy Carter, Ronald Reagan, and George Bush. (See, for example, Bruce 1988, Donovan 1988.) It appears that much of the activity of the more vocal and activist members of the movement arises, at least partially, from the failure of these perceived links to achieve more than the minimal desired changes.

Resource mobilization theory looks at the resources—in terms of money, members, organizations, public support, and other forms of support—a movement has been able to garner over time. It is basically an economic model, assuming that the industrial model of organizations can be applied to social movements. It examines budget changes, memberships, organizational endorsements, the increasing professionalization of organizations, and such as key indicators of the movement's success or failure. Certainly, these are important factors in any movement's ability to persist. These factors will be considered as we examine various sectors of the anti-abortion movement. Resource mobilization theory is most relevant to those sectors of the movement that engage in traditional political activities, seeking changes in laws and regulations.

The conflict, or Marxist, model would view the anti-abortion movement as an expression of class conflict. While the activities of the movement that are most visible—picketing, blockading, and bombing—appear to be dominated by members of the working class, other sectors of the movement are dominated by professional, upper- and middle-class people (Blanchard and Prewitt 1993, Cuneo 1989, Ginsburg 1990, Luker 1984). Different sectors are dominated by different social classes, but the movement as a whole spans all social classes. Thus, the Marxist position has some validity for the anti-abortion movement, but it is not all-encompassing. Social class may have more to do with the *nature* of the participation in the movement—the kind of actions taken—than with the *cause* of participation.

It is my contention that no single theory is sufficient to explain the complexities of any social movement. Those which concentrate on social organizations in movements, the political-economic approaches, for instance, generally overlook the importance of the sociopsychological factors that impel individuals to participate. Thus, I will invoke a number of theories at appropriate stages of the analysis.

Of particular help will be resource mobilization theory. As stated above, this is basically an industrial, or economic, model; as such, it employs the terminology of economics, assessing movement dynamics in terms of *industry, sector,* and *organization.* An organization is a group within a movement with a specific agenda that sets it apart from other groups. Organizations in the anti-abortion movement include the National Right to Life Committee, Operation Rescue, and Lambs for Christ. A movement sector is comparable with manufacturing or government employment in the U.S. economy. In relation to the anti-abortion movement, it would be the New Right of the 1970s and 1980s, which used a number of issues (such as abortion, prayer in schools, pornography, homosexual rights, and sex education in schools) to mobilize a constituency. Thus, a sector includes numerous organizations in a coalition concerned with multiple, related issues. (See, for example, Conway and Siegelman 1984 and Hunter 1991.) The industry would be the movement itself, the whole complex of organizations, with their diverse constituencies, goals, strategies, and tactics. Some organizations in a particular industry are also involved in other industries, or movements. In the case of the anti-abortion movement, for instance, some organizations are involved with anti-nuclear, anti–death penalty, and pro-feminist groups. These links to other issues have implications for movement commitment, support, and the type of activity engaged in. These distinctions help to place events and organizations in a larger context. This broader perspective will help us examine the shifting coalitions within the social movement over time.

Resource mobilization theory does of course have its shortcomings. (See Wilson 1983.) It tends, for example, to ignore the role of the state and other interest groups in controlling movement organizations or encouraging movement organizational coalitions. I add that it also tends to emphasize organizational problems and prospects while paying little attention to the reasons why people form or join organizations in the first place. It tends to stress the rational aspects of individuals and organizations while ignoring or downplaying the roles of emotion and spontaneity (Killian 1972). The sociopsychological approaches help to fill these gaps. One of my contentions in the following pages is that different theoretical perspectives are appropriate to analysis of different levels and types of anti-abortion movement organizations.

Chapter 2

Abortion History: Grounds for the Movement toward Liberalization

This chapter lays out a brief history of the United States' evolving views on abortion through the early 1970s, up to the point when the U.S. Supreme Court made its landmark rulings—*Roe v. Wade* and the lesser-known *Doe v. Bolton.* Particular attention is paid to the numerous social and technological changes that have taken place since the beginning of the twentieth century that laid the ground for the drive to lift restrictions on abortion.

Church Doctrine, Public Policy, and Actual Practice through the Nineteenth Century

Abortion laws in Western civilization arose from the positions among theologians of the Roman Catholic church and the practical situations of pregnant women. Prior to the development of modern medical technology, a woman could not be sure she was pregnant until quickening—when she felt movements from the fetus—usually about the fifth month of pregnancy. A woman's menses could be irregular or delayed for a number of reasons other than pregnancy, and she might experience distension of the abdomen for a number of other causes. She might even use folk and herbal remedies to restore menstrual flow prior to quickening under the assumption that something other than pregnancy was preventing her periods.

Some early church elders condemned the practice of abortion.[1] Among those denouncing it was the *Didache*, an early Christian document, meaning "The Teaching" in Greek (circa A.D. 100); Clement of Alexandria, Athenagoras, Turtullian, and Cyprian in the second century; and Jerome and Augustine in the fourth century. Between 450 and 1450, church doctrine allowed abortion only before quickening. From these early elders to nineteenth-century theologians, the debate over the status of the fetus—essentially whether it was human or prehuman—tended to revolve around the concept of "ensoulment." This debate, by and large, assumed that the fetus was not "human" until it was infused by God with a soul; that is, "formed." Most Catholic theologians believed that ensoulment occurred at the time of quickening.[2] Thus, the practices of women and the positions of the church, as well as the later common law, usually coincided. While theologians developed more or less sophisticated theological arguments about when the fetus became ensouled, the common law tended to take for granted that abortion was, even when illegal, no more than a misdemeanor. It was not defined as murder, and usually only the abortionist was subject to punishment.

Between 1450 and 1750, church teaching generally held to the allowance of abortion before quickening and also allowed it after quickening to save the woman's life. The eighteenth-century Catholic theologian Sanchez also held that abortion was acceptable in cases of rape, of a single woman whose family would kill her for having become pregnant, and of a woman "betrothed to another." Pope Gregory XIII, who led the church from 1572 to 1585, allowed it in the first 40 days of pregnancy and for single women under extenuating circumstances.

Pius IX began a dramatic shift in church policy in 1854 with the affirmation of the Immaculate Conception of Mary, which elevated the status of women—particularly the "sacredness" of their child-bearing role—in church dogma. In 1869 excommunication was declared the punishment for performing an abortion, the ban on abortion was expanded in 1895 even to save the woman's life, and in 1917 excommunication was extended to include the woman. In 1902 the ban was extended to include ectopic pregnancies, and 1931 saw promulgation of a church law banning abortion under any circumstance. Exceptions were allowed in practice, however, where saving the woman's life resulted in the death of the fetus indirectly, as in ectopic pregnancies and cases of uterine cancer (J. T. Noonan 1967). Essentially, abortion of the fetus could not be directly intended, even when the pregnancy threatened the woman's health.

From 1800 to 1850 in the United States, public policy on abortion generally followed British common law, which revolved around the concept of quickening.[3] The first abortion law in the United States, passed in Connecticut in 1821, made abortion illegal only after quickening and seems to have been aimed not at abortion itself but at the use of poisons as abortifacients, which put the life of the woman at risk. By 1841 10 states had passed laws regulating abortion. The 1828 New York law was the first to permit abortion after quickening to save the woman's life and to require the consultation and approval of two physicians. The primary motivation behind these laws was clearly to protect women from the unsafe methods of abortion available at the time rather than to control them or punish them for "immoral behavior." Abortion remained a general practice, and the female subculture maintained a repertoire of abortifacients. Midwives and herbal folk healers in particular preserved an inventory of abortion methods. In addition, there was a wide variety of advertised, over-the-counter medications claiming to "restore female regularity." Documents from the time (1800–1910) indicate that those women seeking abortions were primarily unmarried, as opposed to married women wanting to limit the size of their families.

Despite the 10 laws passed in the first half of the nineteenth century, the first campaign against abortion in the United States did not forcefully arise until about the late 1860s. This campaign arose from four basic sources: the drive for medical professionalization, a call for moralism, concern for women's health, and a mix of social forces stemming from industrialization and mass immigration.

The American Medical Association (AMA) was organized in 1847 as part of medical practitioners' efforts to improve their status. Publicly recognized professionalization has generally required that the occupational group establish, among other things, standards of practice, standards for admission to the profession, and a legally sanctioned exclusive right to perform professional services. One of the AMA's first goals was to make it illegal for nonphysicians, especially midwives, to perform abortions.[4]

The AMA's campaign against abortion was also, as Petchesky (1984:82) maintains, a *moral* campaign aimed at encouraging chastity in women. The rising Victorian morality saw out-of-wedlock pregnancy as punishment for sin, and abortion was a means of escaping deserved public censure. Medical practitioners also sought to limit the growth of immigrant and nonwhite Protestant populations.[5] Involuntary sterilization was practiced on at least 45,000 persons between 1907 and 1945 (Caron 1989).

The moral campaign was fueled by Anthony Comstock, who worked diligently against vice and sin, particularly pornography, sexual license, and abortion. The Comstock Law, passed by Congress in 1872, forbade the use of the U.S. mail to transport obscene art and literature and "any drug, medicine, or article for abortion or contraceptive purpose; forbade their advertisement through the mails, and outlawed their manufacture or sale in the District of Columbia or federal territories." As a special agent for the post office, Comstock had "almost unlimited authority over American vice" and set about cleansing the society (Lader 1966:91). The last quarter of the nineteenth century was at least partially the story of attempts to reinstitute puritanism.

At the same time, medical technology was virtually nonexistent. The use of anesthetics was not introduced until during the Civil War. Antisepsis was still not generally accepted in the profession, resulting in an extremely high rate of death from infections introduced by the surgeons. Thus, when abortions were medically performed there was a high risk of infection and death. Indeed, possibly one of the motivations lying behind the early abortion laws was to protect women from the dangers of the various technologies used, although professionalism and moralism may have held precedence.

Another force behind the drive to make abortion illegal arose from a combination of social factors in the last quarter of the nineteenth century. The industrialization and urbanization of the United States was beginning in earnest. These two trends initiated other changes that may have encouraged the use of abortion.[6]

First, children became less valued. On the family farm children were an economic resource, an extra pair of hands, but in the city they are an economic liability, costing money rather than adding to the family income and production. By 1840 there appeared a decline in the birth rate; between 1810 and 1890 it was cut in half. By the 1850s it became clear that those having abortions also included more and more middle- and upper-class married white Protestant females (Mohr 1978). Second, women, especially young, single women, were increasingly being employed outside the home in wage-earning positions.

Finally, educational achievement was becoming more important for both sexes. The public school movement arose about mid-nineteenth century at least partially to provide better trained workers for the newly industrialized work place.[7] A college education was becoming a prerequisite for entrance into the professions of law, medicine, and the clergy; apprenticeship was on its way out.[8]

As a result of all the above, the American family structure was undergoing change. The expenses of rearing children and educating them and the demands of the work world increasingly called for a small, limited nuclear family. With urbanization and mobility there also came the relative independence of the nuclear family, which could no longer depend on an extended network of relatives or on the community for support in times of need. This development, for example, made Social Security almost a necessity.

All of these changes reflect a developing concern with "quality of life."[9] With regard to abortion, quality of life came to mean more than the quality of the newborn's life; also at issue was the quality of the mother's life—as in the case of a teenager who would be handicapped by rearing an infant as a single mother or of a family that could not or did not want to invest time, money, and emotion in caring for an additional child. Families with severely handicapped children in particular found their financial and emotional resources exhausted by the cost of care. Physicians began to allow more severely handicapped or deformed newborns to die from a lack of attention.

At the same time, immigration was increasing, threatening white Anglo-Saxon Protestant hegemony. The Know Nothing Party and the Ku Klux Klan, among others, arose to oppose the foreign "threat." One of the darkest pockets of U.S. history is the record use of lynching, especially of African-Americans, as means of local social control after the Civil War; it peaked in the 1930s. Another, of which few people are now aware, is the riots against Catholics and various ethnic groups in the late 1800s and early 1900s, such as those in Boston in which churches and convents were burned and nuns and priests killed. The late nineteenth century also saw the rise, primarily in the South, of Jim Crow laws, which limited African-Americans' access to public accommodations, the professions, testifying in court, and public education, as well as laws against interracial marriages. This bigotry also led some Americans to see the practice of abortion by white Anglo-Saxon women as a threat to their survival; they were afraid that the then-dominant white Anglo-Saxon Protestants would soon be outnumbered by such groups as Eastern European Jews and Catholics.[10]

Thus, a coalition of medical professionals, moralists, xenophobics, anti-Catholics, and anti-Semites managed to get the various state legislatures to enact laws restricting abortion. Their campaign was fueled by several widely publicized deaths from abortions, usually performed by medical practitioners. Also, an AMA-sponsored study in 1871 estimated that there were as many as 1 million induced abortions annually (or 20 percent of all pregnancies) in the United States. It is hard to determine, at this date, the validity of this study and its claims. The estimate may be accurate, or it may have been inflated to serve the AMA's professionalization goals. In any case, a number of estimates made at the time concur (see Luker 1984:19). If the AMA study is accurate, the abortion rate of more than 100 years ago is remarkably close to today's. Of course, the profiles of those getting abortions then and now are probably quite different. It is also significant that Kinsey (1954) found that nearly 25 percent of the women he surveyed had had an abortion at some point, a proportion virtually the same as the rates recorded since the 1973 rulings on *Roe v. Wade* and *Doe v. Bolton*.

The Ramifications of Social and Technological Change through the Early 1970s

By 1890 every state had laws regulating and outlawing some types of abortion, with most of the predominantly Catholic states, such as Connecticut and Massachusetts, following the Vatican policy, including the outlawing of the dissemination of birth control. As state laws evolved over the next century, disparities arose among them. Some allowed abortion only to save the woman's life. Others allowed it if the pregnancy and/or delivery threatened her physical health. Still others broadened the definition of health to include mental health. Most states allowed abortion for victims of rape or incest.

From about 1910 through the 1920s, and in later government programs, there were efforts to encourage the use of birth control and even involuntary sterilization among women who were perceived as being "defective"; African-American women and retarded women were targets of these efforts. Nativism thus persisted, accompanied by a desire to curtail the cost of governmental assistance programs to the poor, who were perceived as minorities (Caron 1989).

While individual state laws differed in their comprehensiveness, by 1970 abortion became the only medical procedure in the United States generally requiring various combinations of (1) clearance by a panel of physicians rather than only the individual practitioner, (2) clearance by a psychiatrist, (3) a length of residence in a particular state by the woman seeking the abortion, usually six months, (4) the consent of someone other than the patient, normally her husband or parent, and (5) a unique definition of "informed consent" (Faux 1988:121). (The ruling in *Planned Parenthood v. Casey,* the 1992 Pennsylvania case, for example, requires the physician to inform the patient on fetal development.)

Luker (1984:42 ff.) concludes that physicians had successfully redefined abortion as a *medical* problem as opposed to "a moral, ethical, religious, social, legal, or economic problem," or, I would add, a female problem. On the other hand, abortion was a legal problem since it was surrounded by shifting legal restrictions. And it must have been viewed as a moral and social problem if state legislatures felt compelled to restrict its availability on nonmedical bases.

The late-nineteenth-century ascendancy of science and physicians' identification of themselves as "scientific" added to the sacred aura surrounding their views on abortion. In addition, as Luker also points out, their tendency not to interfere in one another's practice led to practices that were widely disparate.[11] Thus, the decision to abort became a technical one, left to the judgment of the individual practitioner. One result was disparate access to licit abortion, depending on the woman's knowledge of competent liberal physicians and her access to sufficient funds to cover the relatively high cost of having an abortion in a hospital. These conditions naturally favored middle- and upper-class women.[12]

Many women had to find their way through a "black market," going to physicians willing to stretch the law, to blatantly illegal abortionists who generally charged about 10 times what a legal abortion costs today (but still less than the cost of one in a hospital at that time), or to do-it-yourself abortifacients, which were frequently ineffective and life-threatening. The willingness to take such risks reveals the desperation some women felt.

Tribal societies have typically practiced birth control, abortion, and even infanticide and infant/child abandonment, all of which have been practiced in Western civilization as well. Generally, in tribal societies neither the fetus nor the infant was considered fully human until given a name, incorporated into the kinship group, and assigned a social role. If an infant died prior to incorporation, its body would be treated unceremoniously. A continuation of this perspective is reflected in the emphasis in some European societies on a person's name day, as opposed to his or her birthday.

Traditionally, Western society has accorded different levels of "humanness" to fetuses and infants, dependent on their being assigned social roles, at different stages of incorporation into the family. For example, a spontaneous abortion, or early miscarriage, is typically flushed down the toilet. An induced abortion is treated in virtually the same way.[13] An infant who takes at least one or two breaths is treated differently. It receives an infant death certificate and possibly a truncated funeral. If an infant lives long enough for the family to interact with it, it usually receives more recognition, including being named and baptized and given a more complete funeral service. Another indication of the differences in status for fetuses and infants lies in the different kinds of death certificates required. In the first two trimesters of pregnancy, no formal record is required. Death in the last trimester requires a fetal death certificate. Following a live birth, death in the first year of the infant's life requires an infant death certificate. After one year of life, a "normal" death certificate is issued.

In short, in both tribal societies and in contemporary America, the degree of the human status of the fetus and infant has depended on the extent of its incorporation into social interaction with the kinship group, its being given a social role. Recent changes in medical technology, discussed below, have given the fetus a potential social role, that of patient. Incorporation of the fetus in the family is also encouraged by the growing tendency among some sectors of the society, primarily the middle class, to play music for and read to the fetus, frequently termed *bonding* by those who practice it. This usually begins after fetal movements start.

One reason for the medical profession's original campaign to regulate abortion lay in its realization that the technology of the time (1870s) was not safe enough; an intolerable number of women died from the procedure. Thus, one factor in physicians' opposition to abortion was their desire to save women's lives, at least according to their public statements. By the twentieth century many of the conditions that had previously indicated a need for an abortion—tuberculosis, heart and kidney problems, pernicious vomiting—were treatable. Thus, arguments in favor of abortion shifted more to the social and psychological consequences of carrying to term (Luker 1984:54–55). Also, the technology of abortion itself had vastly improved, such that by 1970 having an abortion was far safer than carrying a pregnancy to term.[14]

Technology dealing with the fetus has also improved. Amniocentesis and sonoscanning have made it possible to detect fetal abnormalities as never before. These techniques provide information that has become the basis for decisions to abort, especially in cases of Down's syndrome, sickle-cell anemia, PKU, spina bifida, and other such negative prognoses for the fetus. There are also new medical treatments for the fetus in the womb, even including some forms of surgery; heart surgery was first performed on a fetus in 1990. In short, the fetus has been transformed into a patient. It has been given, for the first time, a social role.[15]

In addition, the 1973 *Roe v. Wade* and *Doe v. Bolton* decisions (discussed in chapter 3) were problematical in that they were based on the medical technology of the time, on the "viability" of the fetus at different stages of pregnancy. That is, a woman was given complete control of her fetus in the first trimester because during that period the fetus is not viable. States were given permission to enforce limited regulation of abortion in the second trimester, to the point of being able to specify the conditions under which an abortion could be performed, because the fetus is nearer to viability, though usually not fully so. During the third trimester, the court held, states could limit abortion to such conditions as threat to the mother's life, since, theoretically, the fetus is then viable.[16] As technology pushes fetal viability back to earlier and earlier stages of pregnancy,[17] *Roe v. Wade* and *Doe v. Bolton* are presumably alterable as well. Our ability to artificially "extend" life even under brain death supports some people's view that the fetus is at all points of development fully human—that is, the fetus need not be able to function apart from its mother to be "human."

There are those who argue that biological life—including fetal life—is not equivalent to human life. The courts have recognized this fact by declaring brain functioning as the baseline for determining death. Callahan (1984), for example, contends that to be fully human one must have psychological and social awareness in addition to biological existence.[18] Technology has invaded at least the social arena by ascribing to the fetus a social role prior to birth, the role of patient, as noted above. There is still some question about when psychological humanity, self-consciousness, develops.

In the 1950s many hospitals moved toward establishing boards of several physicians to approve abortions. Luker (1984:56 ff.) asserts that while the intent may have been to provide legal protection for the doctors performing abortions, the result was to severely decrease and limit the number of legal abortions, since the boards appeared to meet the criteria of the most restrictive member.

By 1973 there was a wide disparity in state laws.[19] Many forbade abortions except to save the woman's life. At the other extreme was New York, which allowed for abortion on demand and had a large number of out-of-staters who could afford it coming in to get abortions. In some states physicians openly defied state laws by providing abortions on demand. In most states that regulated abortions a number of obstetricians and gynecologists quietly provided, in effect, abortions on demand,[20] and abortion was the most frequently performed surgical procedure in the United States. In states restricting abortions underground organizations had developed that referred women to doctors willing to perform illegal abortions.[21]

The establishment of formal organizations[22] was the result, rather than the cause, of changing attitudes toward abortion. After World War II, the United States underwent changes in more than just medical technology. From the 1950s to the 1970s there was a dramatic increase in the demand for professional and other middle-class occupations in the work force. The war had spurred participation of women in the work force, and the GI Bill for veterans and increased prosperity in general led to a larger proportion of both males and females attending and graduating from colleges. Improved standards of living contributed to an increased valuation of "quality of life." Women began delaying marriage, while divorce rates were rising, especially after the initiation of "no fault" divorces, and female-headed households were increasing. Thus, the use of birth control and abortion to limit family size increased dramatically (Petchesky 1984:103).

One important factor leading to the value placed on controlling family size was the development and dissemination of the birth control pill. Giving women a new power of control over their reproduction, the pill may have been a crucial element in further development among many women of the feeling, as never before, that they *should* be able to have complete control over their reproductive lives. Such an ethos leads to the idea that if one method, birth control, fails, other methods, such as abortion, should be available. This ethos was a contributing factor to the "sexual revolution."

Owing to improvements in medical care and hence greater longevity, contemporary women spend a much smaller proportion of their lives mothering children.[23] The combination of improved birth control methods, the sexual revolution, greater longevity, and increased participation of women—married and single—in the work force has led, primarily among those involved in those changes, to a devaluation of the mothering role. Women who place a greater value on their career also tend to look upon their husbands as companions or friends. Children are often perceived as barriers to both career and the husband-wife relationship (Komarovsky 1967).[24]

At the same time, other segments of the population, primarily working class or rural, seemed untouched by the changing ethos. While the majority of working-class women had joined the work force following World War II, this was most often out of necessity, to maintain a family or personal life-style. They tended to place a high value on their role as mothers, see work as a necessary evil, and to appraise their husbands in a utilitarian way, as providers who allow them to devote themselves to mothering (Komarovsky 1967).[25] Thus, two cultures developed after World War II, with contrasting and conflicting views of work, mothering, and marriage. For those highly valuing traditional female roles, the demographic and social changes became a threat, especially the easy availability of birth control, abortion, and no-fault divorce; there is a perception that these developments allow men to forgo their responsibilities to women. (See, for example, publications of Feminists for Life.)

At the same time, there was an almost abrupt change in values regarding population growth. Technologies developed during World War II had also introduced new techniques for controlling major Third World diseases, such as malaria. Insecticides, such as DDT, made it possible to significantly curtail communicable diseases such as malaria. U.N. efforts through the World Health Organization eliminated small pox from the human environment. As a result, the world underwent a "population explosion."[26] Population control became a concern, particularly in middle- and upper-class circles, and received public support. Family planning services, both domestically and internationally, became government funded beginning with the Eisenhower administration in the 1950s, and services were expanded into the 1960s. Indeed, one source of early opposition to John F. Kennedy's candidacy was fear that he would oppose federal funding of family planning and contraception, which he was quick to deny in a campaign speech in Houston. One organization growing out of this general orientation was Zero Population Growth, which was founded in 1968.

Thus, there were a number of sources of support for broader availability and use of birth control and abortion in the years leading up the landmark Supreme Court rulings of *Roe v. Wade* and *Doe v. Bolton* in 1973. These included, at the least, those with "nativist" or racist concerns, the medical profession, some segments of the female population, and those concerned with population control.

Chapter 3

Abortion History: Grounds for the Movement against Abortion

The seeds of the anti-abortion movement lay in the success of the pro-choice movement to reform or repeal restrictive state laws in the 1960s and early 1970s, culminating in the essentially pro-choice Supreme Court decisions of *Roe v. Wade* and *Doe v. Bolton* in 1973. This chapter reviews some of the critical events leading up to the 1973 decisions, describes the decisions themselves and the impact they had on abortion rates, and documents the early response of anti-abortion activists to the plethora of social and legal changes taking place around them. It also briefly encapsulates the White House policy on abortion during the administrations of Jimmy Carter, Ronald Reagan, and George Bush. The combination of ambivalence and encouragement that characterized the White House response to anti-abortion activists for 16 years served to invigorate the movement. Perhaps the most significant legacy of these years is the Supreme Court appointments made by Reagan and Bush. The chapter concludes with a review of the Court's various decisions on abortion-related cases since its rulings on *Roe* and *Doe*.

The Campaign for Abortion Rights through the Early 1970s

In the 1960s abortion rights advocacy was spurred by two events that received widespread coverage by the media. First, the results of the use of thalidomide by pregnant women became known. Use of the drug seemed at first to be largely a concern in Europe, where the birth of more than 8,000 deformed babies were blamed on thalidomide. It became an American issue in 1962 when Sherri Finkbine, a two-months-pregnant Arizona woman, discovered she had taken thalidomide and sought an abortion. Although she had secured the approval of her physician and her hospital, both withdrew their consent in the wake of the publicity surrounding the case; Arizona law permitted abortion only to save the mother's life. Finkbine ultimately went to Sweden for an abortion, but her situation had brought abortion and the states' restrictive laws to national attention.

The second issue arose in 1964 with a national German measles epidemic. Because of the danger of birth defects associated with a woman's contracting German measles during pregnancy,[1] a number of physicians performed more abortions to accommodate pregnant victims of rubella. The disparity between their actual practices and the state laws governing them led some doctors to begin pressuring state legislatures for change. Some state legislatures began supporting the American Law Institute's (ALI) 1959 revision of the abortion section of the Model Penal Code, which became the model for most of the state revisions in the late 1960s. This model law allowed for abortion when pregnancy puts the woman's life or mental health (which is open to wide interpretation) at risk, when pregnancy follows from rape or incest, and when there is fetal deformity. It also required that two physicians approve the abortion.

Organizations that could loosely be qualified as pro-choice varied in the degree of change they sought. Some urged total freedom of choice by women, which meant repeal of all existing restrictions, while most were willing to settle for liberalization of current state restrictions to make it at least easier for most women to get abortions. At the national level there was the Clergyman's Consultation Service on Problem Pregnancies (established in 1967 in New York, it soon had affiliates in other states); a similar organization in Chicago called the Service[2] (also known as Jane, it was reorganized in the late 1980s on a national level to teach do-it-yourself abortion) (Petchesky 1984:28–129)[3]; the National Abortion Rights Action League (NARAL, organized in 1969 as the National Association for the Repeal of Abortion Laws, renamed the National Abortion Rights Action League in 1973); Zero Population Growth (ZPG, 1968); the National Organization for Women (NOW, 1968); and Planned Parenthood (1942, successor to Margaret Sanger's Birth Control League of America, founded in 1922; Sanger's first clinic was established in 1916 in New York City and was the effective beginning of the League). Many of these groups had many causes on their agenda and organized out of prior social concerns, such as the availability of birth control or other women's issues. But as abortion came more to the fore, they added it to their list.

It is difficult to find anyone who is "pro-abortion." Being for the option of abortion is similar to being for the option of appendectomy. Abortion is not likely to arouse in an individual ardent zeal and activism until that person or someone close to him or her feels urgent need of it and feels it would be difficult or impossible to get.[4] It is a latent concern, and it is therefore difficult to organize people behind it as a single issue. To my knowledge there are only three single-issue abortion rights organizations: (1) NARAL, at whose core are professionals engaged in delivering abortions, but which claimed 250,000 members in 1985 (Brozan 1985); (2) the National Abortion Federation (NAF), which is a federation of groups and individuals performing abortions and in 1990 represented 289 clinics and physicians (Kolata 1990:11); and (3) the Religious Coalition for Abortion Rights, an interdenominational organization, many of whose activists have had personal experience—either themselves or through counseling someone else—with abortion.

A number of tactics were used in the late 1960s to press for liberalization of abortion laws. The Chicago clinic Jane performed 11,000 abortions from 1969 to 1973. A physician in California openly performed abortions, defying the judicial system to arrest and try him. Clergy and feminists formed referral services, primarily in the Midwest and East. Abortion activists picketed and invaded AMA conventions, legislative hearings, and courtrooms. Sit-ins at public hospitals and public speak-outs were held (Petchesky 1984:128–29).

Most efforts to liberalize abortion laws took place at the state level and in the more populous and traditionally liberal states. There was, for example, the Wisconsin Committee to Legalize Abortion (1966), Chicago-area Zero Population Growth (1970), Chicago Women's Liberation Union (1969), Chicago NOW (1969), California's Society for Humane Abortions (1966), and New York's Association for the Study of Abortion (1966). Legislative efforts at reform were largely aimed at broadening state laws to include what many physicians were already doing. A number of the more activist groups, however, had a much different agenda, the total repeal of all restrictions on abortion.

In 1970 New York passed the most liberal abortion law in the nation, leaving the decision to the woman and the physician at up to 24 weeks of gestation. By 1970 Hawaii, Alaska, New York, and Washington had repealed their abortion laws, and 12 other states had liberalized theirs.[5] Most had residency requirements of 30–90 days; only New York had no residency requirement (Sarvis and Rodman 1974). These changes had taken place within a period of four short years, from 1967 to 1970.

Because efforts at the state level were so significant to the pro-choice movement—and hence the ferment of the anti-abortion movement—it is worth taking a closer look at them. A good example of the successful effort to reform abortion law at the state level is the experience in California. Events in Hawaii demonstrate a campaign that accomplished repeal, thereby leaving the decision of whether to have an abortion entirely to a woman and her physician.[6]

California and Reform   Efforts toward abortion law reform in California arose from such disparate sources as religious groups (Unitarian, Jewish, and Episcopalian), the American Association of University Women, the American Humanist Association,[7] and the California Junior Chamber of Commerce (Jaycees), among whom the issue was first raised by a physician. Testimony against reform before a legislative committee was primarily from Catholic sources. The broader base of the pro-reform groups seemed to indicate that there was widespread support for change.

Furthermore, between 1964 and 1967 a number of prestigious professional associations passed resolutions favoring reform, including the AMA, the American Bar Association (ABA), the American Academy of Pediatrics, the California Medical Association, and the California Bar Association (Luker 1984:88). Thus, the movement toward abortion reform was carried out largely by professionals, including particularly physicians and attorneys. Physicians were apparently seeking a compromise position on abortion that would allow them to continue to do legally what some had been doing illicitly. But it was obviously their intent to maintain control over the process of deciding whether to abort (Luker 1984).

With what appeared to be the virtually unanimous support of the medical and legal professions, as well as that of mainline Protestant[8] religious spokespersons, in 1967 the California legislature passed a law allowing abortions performed by a physician in a certified hospital to prevent mental or physical harm to the woman. It also included provisions allowing abortion in the cases of rape and incest. Then Governor Ronald Reagan signed the bill after making sure that a provision allowing abortion of deformed fetuses was removed.

During the debates, negotiations, and political maneuverings leading to reform, there arose another voice, a women's organization, the California Committee on Therapeutic Abortion (CCTA), created to support reform. Although the CCTA's voice was lost amid those of the professionals, the group's presence was significant for marking the beginning of the organization of *women* on the issue.

Other efforts, enjoined primarily by women and led by the Society for Humane Abortions (SHA), coalesced around the goal of repealing California's abortion laws. While reform left the basic decision to abort in the hands of the physician, repeal would put that decision solely in the hands of the woman concerned.[9] While the SHA did not carry the day in California, its public programs and the publicity it received served to bring abortion "out of the closet" and open to more public discussion. The dialogue between SHA and the CCTA also served to unify activist women. The combination of networking and publicity brought more women forward to work for change on the sides of both reform and repeal in California. Furthermore, the call for repeal made reform efforts appear more moderate and palatable to the public and the legislature.[10]

In 1969, in *People v. Belous,* the state supreme court ruled that the 1967 abortion law was unconstitutional, based on the right to privacy and the right of a physician to weigh the risks of an abortion against the risks of bearing to term, both foreshadowing *Roe v. Wade* and *Doe v. Bolton.* By 1971 abortions were available virtually on demand in California and both Blue Cross and Medi-Cal, the state welfare program, were covering them (Luker 1984:134).

Hawaii and Repeal　　In March 1970 the Hawaiian abortion law was repealed, "the first time that virtually all restrictions on abortion had been removed by a legislative body" (Steinhoff and Diamond 1977:vii). Beginning in 1967, bills had been introduced in the state legislature both to repeal and to reform (usually in line with the American Law Institute recommendation) the current restrictive laws. These efforts died at various points in the legislative process, but by 1969 reform bills had passed in California, Colorado, and

North Carolina. In 1968 England enacted the broadest reform, allowing consideration of the woman's home situation in the decision to abort.

The 1969 committee in the Hawaii House of Representatives assigned to review the abortion law proposals held hearings at which representatives of the medical association, a number of mainline Protestant denominations, nurses, and others supported reform, half of them also supporting repeal. Opposition came from the Catholic diocese and a Catholic physicians organization. The reform bill passed the House by a 75 percent majority.

State Senate hearings followed a pattern similar to those in the House. Joan Hayes, a representative for the American Association for University Women (AAUW), began leading a movement for repeal. In the ensuing wavering and maneuvering, the session closed without action. But one key senator, Vincent Yano, a Catholic attorney, became convinced of Father Robert Drinan's position, that no abortion law is better than one that condones it in specific circumstances, since then the law condones murder.[11] When the AAUW sponsored a seminar prior to the next legislative session for 200 community leaders, Yano announced that he would introduce repeal at the 1970 session. This initiated a campaign for repeal.

Opposition to repeal came from a House member who favored reform and the officialdom of the Catholic church. A converted Catholic layman, Robert Pearson, rose as leader of the anti-repeal forces. Pearson spoke widely, using visuals of fetuses in his talks and on billboards, which had a negative effect on a number of people.[12]

The arguments raised by the opposition to repeal mirror those which would become standard in the anti-abortion movement (Steinhoff and Diamond 1977): (1) the fetus is fully human; (2) fetal souls are doomed to eternal limbo[13]; (3) fetal life has ultimate precedence over that of mother, if a choice must be made[14]; (4) repeal denies legal protection to the fetus, which is an "innocent" life[15]; (5) women's rights and roles should be limited to and foster their natural function of mothering; (6) repeal would foster sexual permissiveness and irresponsibility; and (7) the fear of pregnancy is a deterrent to sexual misbehavior.

Repeal passed the Hawaii House by a vote of 31 to 20 and the Senate by 15 to 9. Governor J. A. Burns, personally opposed to abortion, allowed the bill to become law without his signature. From 1970 to at least 1976, bills to reverse repeal were introduced in the legislature, but none ever got beyond a committee. Organized public groups in opposition to repeal, such as Hawaii Right to Life, arose primarily after *Roe v. Wade.*

The Response to State Reform and Repeal

Responses to the efforts to reform or repeal state abortion laws appear to have begun with the National Catholic Bishops' appointment of their Family Life Bureau in May 1967, following the passage of abortion law reform in three states. Soon there were indictments against persons engaged in abortion and abortion referrals in four states.[16] Elsewhere, during the first campaigns for reform and repeal, small anti-abortion groups did organize, but it was not until reform and repeal legislation was passed that more serious, concerted counteraction took place. In California, for example, the opposition to reform was caught off guard. A small group of professionals, primarily males, did organize, but they seemed to assume that all they had to do was to state the case for the humanity of the fetus and most people would agree with them; they underestimated the force of the movement for reform and repeal. Physicians and social workers—people who were likely to "bump into" the abortion debate through their work—also got involved in the anti-abortion movement in the late 1960s and early 1970s. Most early anti-abortion efforts were initiated and sponsored by officials of the Roman Catholic church, which may have inhibited their growth beyond Catholic circles. It was not until about 1971, after three to four years of reform, that it became clear how many abortions were actually being performed (Luker 1984). Concerted opposition to abortion beyond the state level did not develop until shortly after the *Roe v. Wade* and *Doe v. Bolton* Supreme Court decisions in 1973.

Roe v. Wade and *Doe v. Bolton*

The 1973 Supreme Court decision regarding abortion has become generally known as *Roe v. Wade.* In reality there were two decisions, and the second, *Doe v. Bolton,* was as crucial as—if not more so—than the first.

Roe v. Wade resulted from the efforts of a Texas woman, who claimed she had been raped while working in Georgia with a circus, to obtain an abortion. Norma McCorvey, the Roe of the case, later went public to support the 1973 decision. As the case traveled through the Texas state courts to the U.S. Supreme Court, much time passed and McCorvey's pregnancy proceeded. She eventually decided to have the baby, and so the question of abortion for her as an individual became moot. The issues her case raised, of course, remain significant to this day.

In regard to this case, the majority opinion, delivered by Justice Harry Blackmun, determined that it was "doubtful that abortion was ever firmly established as a common-law crime even with the destruction of a quick fetus." The decision was based primarily on the right to privacy, drawing on the Fourteenth and Ninth Amendments to the Constitution. While the right to privacy is not explicitly mentioned in the Constitution, the Supreme Court had first asserted it under the penumbra of the totality of constitutional intent in the 1965 *Griswold v. Connecticut* decision, which declared unconstitutional the state's right to forbid the sale or use of contraceptives.[17]

Roe did hold, however, that the state could control abortion in some instances. In essence, the decision was based on pregnancy trimesters. During the first trimester the state could not regulate abortion in any way. In the second trimester the state could, if it wished, regulate abortion, but to protect the life or health of the woman, not the fetus. During the third trimester, when the fetus was near viability or actually viable, the state could limit and regulate abortions to protect the fetus. This parallels, more or less, the historical Catholic position based on quickening and the tradition of English/American common law.

Doe v. Bolton, decided at the same time as *Roe v. Wade,* arose from Georgia. Doe's real name was never made public, so little is known of her personal circumstances. But the Court used Doe to detail what kinds of regulations the state could not use in controlling abortions. For example, the *Doe* decision "struck down hospital licensing requirements, a residency requirement, and a requirement that two physicians certify a woman's need to undergo an abortion" (Faux 1988:310). Both decisions, however, basically upheld that while the woman had a right to seek an abortion, the final decision would still be based on a *physician's* professional judgment, thereby affirming that most of the bureaucratic and other restrictions on abortion interfered with "the physician's right to practice" (*Doe v. Bolton,* p. 199, cited in Petchesky 1984:291). Thus both *Roe v. Wade* and *Doe v. Bolton* upheld the professional status medical practitioners had sought when severe restrictions on abortion were first put into place in the nineteenth century. The court specifically stated, "a pregnant woman does not have an absolute constitutional right to an abortion on her demand" *(Doe v. Bolton,* 410 U.S. 1979 [1973], p. 9).

Furthermore, the use of fetal viability as the swing point in determining the moment at which the state may intervene and restrict abortions presents myriad difficulties. As Faux (1988:322 ff.) indicates, (1) viability varies from fetus to fetus, (2) the earlier the birth the higher the risk of severe abnormalities, such as blindness and learning disabilities, and (3) viability opens the door to fetal rights. In addition, the use of fetal viability begs the question of what valid interest the state has in potential life and of how far it may go in protecting that life.

One effect of the 1973 decisions, which took effect immediately, was the nullification of virtually every state law dealing with abortion. Thirty-one states having restrictive laws, in effect, were left with no valid law. Even the four states that had repealed their abortion laws still had some restrictions, such as residency requirements, and those provisions became unconstitutional (Faux 1988:326).

Roe and *Doe* left a number of unanswered questions, most of which were to arise in the next two decades. Left pending were parental consent requirements for minors, informed consent of the woman, spousal consent, possible reporting requirements, possible regulation of the types of procedures to be used, advertising of abortion services, the possibility of nonphysicians performing abortions, and the freedom of choice for private hospitals to forgo performing abortions. Related issues include the experimental and medical use of fetuses, waiting periods, termination of parental rights, the right of a physician to refuse to perform abortions, notice requirements, and government funding of abortions (Lewis *et al.* 1981).

Effects of the Supreme Court Decisions on Abortion Rates

While it is fairly easy to ascertain the trends in the increase in *legal* abortions that resulted from the Supreme Court decisions, it is difficult to determine whether there has been an increase in the *total* number of abortions, both legal and illegal, since 1973. Records of illegal abortions, of course, are not kept. It is estimated that about 1 million illegal abortions were performed per year prior to 1973, with 100,000 of those resulting in hospital admission from perforation or hemorrhage. Illegal abortions were the major cause of maternal death prior to 1973 (Irwin 1970:21). Analysis is complicated by a dramatic increase in the percentage of persons using contraceptives; 0.2 percent per year from 1965 through 1969 and 3.0 percent per year from 1973 to 1980. At the same time, by 1976, 64 percent of unmarried sexually active teenagers were using contraceptives (Zelnik and Kantner 1977; cited in Jaffe *et al.* 1981). Thus, there was a decrease over that period in the number of unwanted pregnancies.

Another factor is that the legalization of abortion dramatically reduces the cost, making it more financially available to more women, particularly those of lower-income groups. I conclude from various readings and interviews related to previous research that a legal abortion in a clinic or physician's office costs about one-tenth that of an illegal abortion or one conducted in a hospital operating room, as required under the majority of state laws prior to 1973.[18] The greater availability of abortions—financially, geographically, and legally—is a significant factor in expecting a spectacular increase in abortion rates.[19]

Today, approximately one-third of all known pregnancies are terminated through induced abortions (Alan Guttmacher Institute; Center for Disease Control).[20] The number of legal abortions in the United States since the 1973 court decisions has ranged consistently between 1.3 and 1.5 million per year, with a slight annual decline since 1988. About one-third are teenagers, another third aged 20–24, and the rest over age 25. Teenagers had about one-half the rate of legal abortions in 1972 (most in New York and California) as they have had since 1980. Two-thirds of those seeking abortions in the years since 1980 were unmarried. The percentage of nonwhite women getting legal abortions more than tripled between 1972 and 1977 (Jaffe *et al.* 1981:11).[21] Nonetheless, the average woman getting an abortion is young, white, and unmarried (Alan Guttmacher Institute).

Coming at the problem from another side, it is estimated that about one-half of all pregnancies are unintended or unwanted and that about one third of those were aborted illegally prior to 1973, while approximately 75 percent of them are currently aborted (Jaffe *et al.* 1981:14–16, Alan Guttmacher Institute).

While it is clear to researchers that there has been an increase in abortion rates, it is not as great as anti-abortionists claim. The evidence is also relatively clear that abortion is not being used as a primary means of birth control but is most frequently the result of failed contraceptives (Jaffe *et al.* 1981, Alan Guttmacher Institute) or the culturally induced bias of some working- and lower-class men and women against the use of contraceptives.[22]

The Response to *Roe v. Wade* and *Doe v. Bolton*

The primary anti-abortion organizations existing prior to the Supreme Court decisions of 1973 were Catholic—national, diocesan, and even local parish family life or right to life committees—and so the earliest reactions to those decisions were primarily Catholic.[23] The Catholic Bishops' Conference began allocating larger monies to national right to life efforts, as did various dioceses, depending on the sentiments of particular bishops.[24] At their spring meeting in 1973 they made these recommendations to the National Catholic Conference: (1) organize right to life groups in every state, (2) call on dioceses to fund church and ecumenical anti-abortion endeavors, (3) help the National Right to Life Association in any possible way, and (4) use one day each month for prayer and fasting in "reparation" for abortions (Faux 1988:328–29).

An immediate response to the Supreme Court decisions was a deluge of protesting letters to the Court itself, which Faux (1988:328) maintains were the result of an organized effort. A concomitant effort was a letter campaign to congressmen and senators at Easter. The Catholic effort included a Committee of Ten Million, which sponsored a petition campaign to Congress for a human rights amendment.

Various "human life amendments" were introduced in both houses of Congress, the most persistent one over the years seeking to protect the fetus from the point of conception onward. None to date has been approved. Other restrictive efforts at the national level were more successful. In October 1973 Senator Jesse Helms (Republican, North Carolina) managed to add an amendment to the Foreign Aid Bill that forbade the use of U.S. funds for abortions and abortifacients. Beginning in 1977, Senator Henry Hyde (Republican, Illinois) introduced bills limiting the use of public funds for abortions; since 1980 federal funds have been made available only in cases of rape, incest, and life-saving abortions.[25] In general, efforts to pass restrictive laws have had more success at the state level.

Despite the coordinated response of the Catholic church, most Americans with anti-abortion sentiments seem to have been caught off guard by 1973 Supreme Court decisions. Current research on anti-abortion activists may cast some light on the apparent naivete of that assumption. Some research in the 1980s on those involved in the more activist segments of the anti-abortion movement (see, for example, Blanchard and Prewitt 1993, Himmelstein 1986, and Luker 1984) indicates that they tend to have limited and circumscribed social relationships.[26] Most are Protestant fundamentalists extremely active in their churches and associated religious organizations who tend not to interact significantly with those of differing worldviews. Thus, most of the feedback they get from others reinforces their views.[27] This relative social and psychological isolation may account for the surprise certain segments of the anti-abortion population felt upon the rulings in *Roe* and *Doe*.

The White House on Abortion since *Roe* and *Doe*

Social movements frequently find themselves in opposition to the existing social order, especially to the public policies that codify that order. The separation of powers among the legislative, judicial, and executive branches of government in the United States, however, makes it possible to enlist one or more branches of government against another. A movement that succeeds in such an effort has the advantage of adding to itself an increased aura of legitimacy in the public arena. Getting one branch of government on its side also helps to create an atmosphere in which success seems within reach, a decided enhancement in recruiting additional adherents.

Since *Roe v. Wade* and *Doe v. Bolton,* each president has involved himself to some degree in the abortion issue since. In August 1977 Jimmy Carter cut off Medicaid funds for abortions except in cases of danger to the woman's life (*60 Minutes,* 14 August 1977). Ronald Reagan involved himself more than any other president, clearly giving the anti-abortion movement an aura of legitimacy. He sent an anti-abortion delegation to the United Nations World Conference in Mexico City in 1984; he entertained a delegation of anti-abortion leaders at the White House; he approved the 1984 Hyde Amendment, thereby forbidding the allocation of federal funds to international family planning organizations promoting abortion; he banned the importation of the so-called abortion pill, RU-486; and he forbade the use of fetal tissue in medical research involving federal funds.[28] The Bush administration largely continued to support Reagan's policies. Bush did initiate a ban on mentioning abortion in federally funded abortion counseling in 1991, which he revised in 1992, giving physicians—but no other staff members—the right to discuss it with patients. He also vetoed the freedom of choice bill, which would have made the provisions of *Roe* and *Doe* statutory law. (The abortion-related actions and policies of the Carter, Reagan, and Bush administrations are discussed in detail in chapter 6; actions and policies of the early Clinton administration are discussed in chapter 9.)

The most significant legacy of both administrations, however, is their appointments to the Supreme Court. Between them Reagan and Bush nominated five justices: Sandra Day O'Connor, Reagan's only appointee, joined the Court in 1981; Antonin Scalia joined in 1986, Anthony Kennedy in 1988, David H. Souter in 1990, and Clarence Thomas in 1991. Those appointments led to the majority that issued the *Webster v. Reproductive Health Services* decision in 1989 and the Pennsylvania decision in 1992 (described below), both of which have had the effect of curtailing a woman's right to an abortion.

Supreme Court Cases since *Roe* and *Doe*

The advertisement of abortion services was determined to be constitutional in *Bigelow v. Virginia* in 1975.

The Court determined in *Connecticut v. Menillo* in 1975 that states could allow only physicians to perform abortions (Lewis *et al.* 1981:8). (At the time some abortifacients were sold as patent medicines.)

The first case to test the limits of the 1973 decisions was *Planned Parenthood of Central Missouri v. Danforth* in 1976.[29] The Court determined that requiring a physician to get the written informed consent of the patient after informing her of the dangers and alternatives was permissible. In the same case, the Court held unconstitutional the requirement of spousal consent and of a woman under the age of 18 to secure her parents' consent, since the law did not provide minors with other avenues, such as securing a judge's permission. (The Court later upheld parental consent laws, as long as minors were offered alternative avenues, in *Belotti v. Baird* [1979] and *Planned Parenthood of Kansas City v. Ashcroft* [1983].[30]) State requirements that doctors report to the state information on each abortion were upheld on condition that the reports relate to maternal health and be held in confidence. *Danforth*'s banning of saline abortions was rejected, as were its statutes attempting to protect pre-viable fetuses (Lewis *et al.* 1981:5–6).

In *Poelker v. Doe, Beal v. Doe,* and *Maher v. Roe,* all heard in 1977, the Court held that government entities could refuse to perform or fund elective abortions in public hospitals.[31]

In 1979 the Court ruled in *Collauti v. Franklin* that a Pennsylvania law requiring a physician to predict the fetus's viability was too vague. (In 1983, however, in *Planned Parenthood of Kansas City v. Ashcroft,* it upheld a Missouri provision requiring the presence of a second physician in all post-viable abortions; that is, abortions in which the fetus could be viable if delivered naturally or by caesarean.)

In 1980, in *Harris v. McRae,* the Court upheld the Hyde Amendment, which forbids the use of federal funds for abortions.

In 1981, the Court approved a Utah requirement that a doctor notify the parents of a minor that she is seeking an abortion when she is (1) dependent on and living with the parents, (2) not emancipated or married, and (3) has not sought a judicial approval (Lewis *et al.* 1981:7).

In the *Webster* decision of 1989, the Supreme Court upheld, technically, *Roe* and *Doe,* while at the same time allowing states to regulate abortions, even in the first trimester, contrary to *Roe* and *Doe.* The virtual effect of the decision was to give states the freedom to enact laws impeding totally free choice and access to abortion. It allowed for (1) fetal viability tests; (2) requirements for parental consent in the case of minors if alternative avenues were provided for them, such as a judge's permission; (3) prohibition of the use of public facilities, including hospitals, and public funds in the performance of abortions; and (4) regulation of clinics performing abortions.

The scene thus shifted back to the states and the passage of laws to limit and regulate abortions at that level to chip away at *Roe* and *Doe.* The *Webster* decision had the effect of reawakening both sides at the state level. Anti-abortion efforts shifted to passing state limitations within the framework of *Webster* or even moving beyond those guidelines to overturn *Roe* and *Doe* completely. Pro-choice forces mobilized to try to defeat such efforts. Important limitations were passed in Utah, Louisiana, Guam, and Pennsylvania.

The first of these cases, *Planned Parenthood of Southeastern Pennsylvania v. Casey,* was decided in 1992. While again reaffirming *Roe* and *Doe* and the fundamental right of women to abortion, the justices also, by a 5–4 majority, held that women may be required to hear about fetal development and to wait 24 hours after receiving that information before actually receiving the abortion. Also, the court upheld the right of the state to require physicians to keep detailed records on each performed abortion, records that could be subject to public disclosure. Lastly, they approved requiring minor females to get the consent of one parent or of a state judge. The only Pennsylvania provision the Court rejected was the requirement that married women inform their husbands of their intentions to get an abortion (*Pensacola News Journal*, 30 June 1992).

An interesting explanation for the rigorous efforts of various factions in the anti-abortion movement to make abortion illegal is that the legality of abortion is more important to them than its availability; that is, they resent the stamp of moral approval the law lends to abortion. Blanchard and Prewitt (1993), for example, point to the general availability of abortions on demand prior to 1973 and the general lack of interest fundamentalists then expressed in them. I conclude that fundamentalists are more concerned with the *legitimacy* of abortion than they are with its actual practice.[32]

Chapter 4

Motivation and Ideology: What Drives the Anti-Abortion Movement

For the nearly three decades in which the anti-abortion movement has been active, a variety of individuals and organizations have influenced both the form and the intensity of its protest. This chapter looks at some of the determining factors in movement participation, particularly at what have become perhaps the most important influences in the 1980s and early 1990s—religious and cultural fundamentalism.

Why and How People Join the Anti-Abortion Movement

Researchers have posited a variety of explanations for what motivates people to join the anti-abortion movement. As with any other social movement, the anti-abortion movement has within it various subgroups, or organizations, each of which attracts different kinds of participants and expects different levels of participation. (See Zald and McCarthy 1977 and Staggenborg 1988.) It might in fact be more appropriate to speak of anti-abortion *movements*.

Those opposing abortion are not unified. Some organizations have a single-issue orientation, opposing abortion alone, while others take what they consider to be a "pro-life" stance on many issues, opposing abortion as well as euthanasia, capital punishment, and the use of nuclear and chemical arms. The importance of abortion varies among the latter groups. There are also paper organizations, having virtually no real membership beyond a single organizer and perhaps several persons willing to lend their names to a letterhead. These are usually front groups for other organizations, designed to address topical issues; Defenders of the Defenders of Life, for instance, served the sole purpose of issuing press releases in defense of persons being tried for arsons and bombings. Some organizations arise and die, wax and wane over time as the climate surrounding an issue—in this case, abortion—changes. The rise, demise, and multiplication of various movement organizations can indicate the overall state of the movement: from growing public support and strength to desperation arising from a lack of support. Organizations also differ on goals, tactics, and strategies. The result of all of this differentiation is that various organizations may distance themselves from one another, depending on the disparities between their missions and their means of fulfilling those missions.[1]

Just as the organizations within a movement differ, so do individuals vary in their motivations for joining it. Some anti-abortion activists are clearly anti-feminist, while others act out of communitarian, familistic, or even feminist concerns. Some are motivated by personal history, while others act on the basis of philosophical principle. A combination of factors in an individual's life history and social background contributes to the decision to join the movement in general and to participate in one organization in particular.

Researchers have identified a number of pathways for joining the anti-abortion movement. Luker, in her 1984 study of the early California movement, found that activists in the initial stages of the movement found their way to it through professional associations. The earliest opponents of abortion liberalization were primarily physicians and attorneys who disagreed with their professional associations' endorsement of abortion reform. It is my hypothesis that membership in organizations that concentrate on the education of the public or religious constituencies and on political lobbying is orchestrated primarily through professional networks. With the passage of the California reform bill and the increase in abortion rates several years later, many recruits to the movement fell into the category Luker refers to as "self-selected"; that is, they were not recruited through existing networks but sought out or sometimes formed organizations through which to express their opposition.[2]

Himmelstein (1984), in summarizing the research on the anti-abortion movement available in the 10 years following *Roe v. Wade,* concluded that religious networks were the primary source of recruitment. Religious networks appear to be more crucial in the recruitment of persons into high-profile and/or violence prone groups (Blanchard and Prewitt 1992)—of which Operation Rescue is an example—than into the earlier, milder activist groups (although such networks are generally important throughout the movement). Such networks were also important, apparently, in recruitment into local Right to Life Committees, sponsored by the National Right to Life Committee and the Catholic church. The National Right to Life Committee, for example, is 72 percent Roman Catholic (Granberg 1981). It appears that the earliest anti-abortion organizations were essentially Catholic and dependent on church networks for their members; the recruitment of Protestants later on has also been dependent on religious networks (Cuneo 1989, Maxwell 1992).

Other avenues for participation in the anti-abortion movement opened up through association with other issues. Feminists for Life, for example, was founded by women involved in the feminist movement. Sojourners, a socially conscious evangelical group concerned with issues such as poverty and racism, has an anti-abortion position. Some anti-nuclear and anti-death-penalty groups have also been the basis for the organization of anti-abortion efforts.

Clearly, pre-existing networks and organizational memberships are crucial in initial enlistment into the movement. Hall (1993) maintains that individual mobilization into a social movement requires the conditions of attitudinal, network, and biographical availability. My conclusions regarding the anti-abortion movement support this contention. Indeed, biographical availability—the interaction of social class, occupation, familial status, sex, and age—is particularly related to the type of organization with which and the level of activism at which an individual will engage.[3]

General social movement theory places the motivation to join the anti-abortion movement into four basic categories: status defense; anti-feminism; moral commitment; and cultural fundamentalism, or defense.

The earliest explanation for the movement was that participants were members of the working class attempting to shore up, or defend, their declining social status. (See, for example, Gusfield 1963 and Lorentzen 1980.) Clarke, in his 1987 study of English anti-abortionists, finds this explanation to be inadequate, as do Wood and Hughes in their 1984 investigation of an anti-pornography movement group.

Petchesky (1984) concludes that the movement is basically anti-feminist—against the changing status of women. From this position, the primary goal of the movement is to "keep women in their place" and, in particular, to make them suffer for sexual "libertinism." Statements by some anti-abortion activists support this theory. Cuneo (1989), for example, finds what he calls "sexual puritans" on the fringe of the anti-abortion movement in Toronto. Abortion opponent and long-time right-wing activist Phyllis Schlaffley states this position: "It's very healthy for a young girl to be deterred from promiscuity by fear of contracting a painful, incurable disease, or cervical cancer, or sterility, or the likelihood of giving birth to a dead, blind, or brain-damaged baby (even ten years later when she may be happily married)" (Planned Parenthood pamphlet, no title, n.d. [1990]).

Judie Brown, president of the American Life League, offers this judgment in "The Human Life Amendment" (n.d.):

The woman who is raped has a right to resist her attacker. But the preborn child is an innocent non-aggressor who should not be killed because of the crime of the father. More to the point, since a woman has a right to resist the rapist, she also has the right to resist his sperm. . . . However, once the innocent third party to a rape, the preborn child, is conceived, he should not be killed. . . . Incest is a voluntary act on the woman's part. If it were not, it would be rape. And to kill a child because of the identity of his father is no more proper in the case of incest than it is in the case of rape. (18)

A number of researchers have concluded that sexual moralism is the strongest predictor of anti-abortion attitudes. (See, for example, Woodrum and Davison 1992.)

The theory of moral commitment proposes that movement participants are motivated by concern for the human status of the fetus. It is probably as close as any explanation comes to "pure altruism." Although there is a growing body of research on altruism, researchers on the abortion issue have tended to ignore this as a possible draw to the movement, while movement participants almost exclusively claim this position: that since the fetus is incapable of defending itself, they must act on its behalf.

In examining and categorizing the motivations of participants in the anti-abortion movement in Toronto, Cuneo (1989:85ff.) found only one category—civil rights—that might be considered altruistic. The people in this category tend to be nonreligious and embarrassed by the activities of religious activists; they feel that fetuses have a right to exist but cannot speak for themselves.[4] Cuneo's other primary categories of motivation are characterized by concerns related to the "traditional" family, the status of women in the family, and religion.[5] He also finds an activist fringe composed of what he calls religious seekers; sexual therapeutics, "plagued by guilt and fear of female sexual power" (115); and punitive puritans, who want to punish women for sexual transgressions. All of Cuneo's categories of participant, with the exception of the civil rights category, seek to maintain traditional male/female hierarchies and statuses. If we can generalize Cuneo's Toronto sample to the U.S. anti-abortion movement, I conclude that the majority, but by no means all, of those involved in the movement act out of self-interest, particularly out of defense of a cultural fundamentalist position.

The theory of cultural fundamentalism, or defense, proposes that the anti-abortion movement is largely an expression of the desire to return to what its proponents perceive to be "traditional culture." (See, for example, Blanchard and Prewitt 1993; Clarke 1987; Granberg 1978, 1982; Hunter 1991; Leahy *et al.* 1983; Moen 1984; Page and Clelland 1978; and Wood and Hughes 1984.) This theory incorporates elements of the status defense and anti-feminist theories.

It is important to note that a number of researchers at different points in time (Cuneo 1989; Ginsburg 1990; Luker 1984; Maxwell 1991, 1992) have indicated that (1) there have been changes over time in who gets recruited into the movement and why, (2) different motivations tend to bring different kinds of people into different types of activism, and (3) even particular movement organizations draw different kinds of people with quite different motivations. At this point in the history of the anti-abortion movement, the dominant motivation, particularly in the more activist organizations such as Operation Rescue, appears to be cultural fundamentalism. Closely informing cultural fundamentalism are the tenets of religious fundamentalism, usually associated with certain Protestant denominations but also evident in the Catholic and Mormon faiths. It is to the topics of religious and cultural fundamentalism as they relate to the anti-abortion movement that the large part of this book is devoted and that we now turn.

Religious and Cultural Fundamentalism Defined

Cultural fundamentalism is in large part a protest against cultural change: against the rising status of women; against the greater acceptance of "deviant" life-styles such as homosexuality; against the loss of prayer and Bible reading in the schools; and against the increase in sexual openness and freedom. Wood and Hughes (1984) describe cultural fundamentalism as "adherence to traditional norms, respect for family and religious authority, asceticism and control of impulse. Above all, it is an unflinching and thoroughgoing moralistic outlook on the world; moralism provides a common orientation and common discourse for concerns with the use of alcohol and pornography, the rights of homosexuals, 'pro-family' and 'decency' issues" (89). The theologies of Protestants and Catholics active in the anti-abortion movement—many of whom could also be termed fundamentalists—reflect these concerns.

Protestant fundamentalism arose in the 1880s as a response to the use by Protestant scholars of the relatively new linguistic techniques of text and form criticism in their study of the Bible.[6] These scholars determined that the Pentateuch was a compilation of at least five separate documents written from differing religious perspectives.[7] Similar techniques applied to the New Testament questioned the traditionally assigned authorship of many of its books. The "mainline" denominations of the time (Episcopalian, Congregational, Methodist, Unitarian, and some Presbyterian) began to teach these new insights in their seminaries. With these approaches tended to go a general acceptance of other new and expanding scientific findings, such as evolution.

By 1900 the urbanization and industrialization of the United States were well under way, with their attendant social dislocations. One response to this upheaval was the Social Gospel movement, which strove to enact humanitarian laws regulating such things as child labor, unions, old-age benefits, and guaranteed living wages.[8] With the Social Gospel movement and the acceptance of new scientific discoveries tended to go an optimism about the perfectibility of human nature and society.

Fundamentalism solidified its positions in opposition to these trends as well as in response to social change and the loss of the religious consensus, which came with the influx of European Jewish and Catholic immigrants to America. While fundamentalism was a growing movement prior to 1900, its trumpet was significantly sounded with the publication in 1910 of the first volume of a 12-volume series titled *The Fundamentals*.[9] Prior to the 1920s and 1930s, it was primarily a movement of the North; growth in the South came mostly after 1950.

There are divisions within Protestant fundamentalism, but there is a general common basis of belief. Customary beliefs include a personal experience of salvation; verbal inspiration and literal interpretation of scriptures as worded in the King James Bible; the divinity of Jesus; the literal, physical resurrection of Jesus; special creation of the world in six days, as opposed to the theory of evolution; the virgin birth of Jesus; and the substitutionary atonement (Jesus' death on the cross as a substitution for each of the "saved"). The heart of Protestant fundamentalism is the literal interpretation of the Bible[10]; secondary to this is the belief in substitutionary atonement.

Fundamentalists have also shown a strong tendency toward separatism—separation from the secular world as much as possible and separation from "apostates" (liberals and nonfundamentalist denominations). They are also united in their views on "traditional" family issues: opposing abortion, divorce, the Equal Rights Amendment, and civil rights for homosexuals.[11] While their separatism was expressed prior to the 1970s in extreme hostilities toward Roman Catholicism, fundamentalists and Catholics share a large set of family values, which has led to their pragmatic cooperation in the anti-abortion movement.[12]

Another tie between some Protestant fundamentalists and some Catholics lies in the Charismatic Renewal Movement. This movement, which coalesced in the 1920s (Harrell 1975), emphasized glossolalia (speaking in tongues) and faith healing. Charismatics were denied admission to the World's Christian Fundamental Association in 1928 because of these emphases. By the 1960s charismaticism began spreading to some mainline denominations and Catholic churches. While Presbyterians, United Methodists, Disciples of Christ, Episcopalians, and Lutherans sometimes reluctantly accepted this new charismatic movement, Southern Baptists and Churches of Christ adamantly opposed it, especially the speaking in tongues. But the Catholic charismatics have tended to be quite conservative both theologically and socially, giving them ideological ties with the charismatic Protestant fundamentalists and fostering cooperation between the two in interdenominational charismatic conferences, a prelude to cooperation in the anti-abortion movement.

There is also a Catholic "fundamentalism," which may or may not be charismatic and which centers on church dogma rather than biblical literalism, the Protestant a priori dogma. Catholic fundamentalists accept virtually unquestioningly the teachings of the church.[13] They share with Protestant fundamentalists the assumption that dogma precedes and supersedes analytical reason, while in liberal Catholic and

Protestant thought and in the nation's law reason supersedes dogma. Similar to Catholic fundamentalism is the Mormon faith (or the Church of Jesus Christ of Latter Day Saints), which also takes church dogma at face value.[14]

There are at least six basic commonalities to what can be called Protestant, Catholic, and Mormon fundamentalisms: (1) an attitude of certitude—that one may know the final truth, which includes antagonism to ambiguity; (2) an external source for that certitude—the Bible or church dogma; (3) a belief system that is at root dualistic; (4) an ethic based on the "traditional" family; (5) a justification for violence; and, therefore, (6) a rejection of modernism (secularization). (I am not alone in this position; see Steinfels 1988).

Taking those six commonalities point-by-point:

1. The certitude of fundamentalism rests on dependence on an external authority. That attitude correlates with authoritarianism, which includes obedience to an external authority, and, on that basis, the willingness to assert authority over others.[15]

2. While the Protestant fundamentalists accept their particular interpretation of the King James Version of the Bible as the authoritative source, Mormon and Catholic fundamentalists tend to view church dogma as authoritative.

3. The dualism of Catholics, Protestants, and Mormons includes those of body/soul, body/mind, physical/spiritual.[16] More basically, they see a distinction between God and Satan, the forces of good and evil. In the fundamentalist worldview, Satan is limited and finite; he can be in only one place at one time. He has servants, however, demons who are constantly working his will, trying to deceive believers. A most important gift of the Spirit is the ability to distinguish between the activities of God and those of Satan and his demons.[17]

4. The "traditional" family in the fundamentalist view of things has the father as head of the household, making the basic decisions, with the wife and children subject to his wishes. Obedience is stressed for both wives and children. Physical punishment is generally approved for use against both wives and children.

This "traditional" family with the father as breadwinner and the mother as homemaker, together rearing a large family, is really not all that traditional. It arose on the family farm, prior to 1900, where large numbers of children were an economic asset. Even then, women were essential in the work of the farm. As explained in chapter 3, in the urban environment, the "traditional" family structure was an option primarily for the middle and upper classes, and they limited their family size even prior to the development of efficient birth control methods. Throughout human history women have usually been breadwinners themselves, and the "traditional" family structure was not an option.

5. The justification for violence lies in the substitutionary theory of the atonement theology of both Protestants and Catholics.[18] In this theory, the justice of God demands punishment for human sin. This God also supervises a literal hell, the images of which come more from Dante's *Inferno* than from the pages of the Bible.[19] Fundamentalism, then, worships a violent God and offers a rationale for human violence (such as Old Testament demands for death when adultery, murder, and other sins are committed).[20] The fundamentalist mindset espouses physical punishment of children, the death penalty, and the use of nuclear weapons; fundamentalists are more frequently wife abusers, committers of incest, and child abusers. (See, for example, Brinkerhoff and Pupri 1988 and Pollock and Steele 1968).

6. Modernism entails a general acceptance of ambiguity, contingency, probability (versus certitude), and a unitary view of the universe; that is, the view that there is no separation between body and soul, physical and spiritual, body and mind (when the body dies, the self is thought to die with it). Rejection of modernism and postmodernism is inherent in the rejection of a unitary worldview in favor of a dualistic worldview. The classic fundamentalist position embraces a return to religion as the central social institution, with education, the family, economics, and politics serving religious ends, fashioned after the social structure characteristic of medieval times.[21]

Also characteristic of Catholic, Protestant, and Mormon fundamentalists are a belief in individualism (which supports a naive capitalism); pietism; a chauvinistic Americanism (among some fundamentalists) that sees the United States as the New Israel and its inhabitants as God's new chosen people; and a general opposition to intellectualism, modern science, the tenets of the Social Gospel, and communism. (Some liberal Christians may share some of these views.) Amid this complex of beliefs and alongside the opposition to evolution, interestingly, is an underlying espousal of social Darwinism,[22] the "survival of the fittest" ethos that presumes American society to be truly civilized, the pinnacle of social progress. This nineteenth-century American neocolonialism dominates the contemporary political views held by the religious right. It is also inherent in their belief in individualism and opposition to social welfare programs.[23]

Particular personality characteristics also correlate with the fundamentalist syndrome: authoritarianism, self-righteousness, prejudice against minorities, moral absolutism (a refusal to compromise on perceived moral issues), and anti-analytical, anti-critical thinking. Many fundamentalists refuse to accept ambiguity as a given in moral decision making and tend to arrive at simplistic solutions to complex problems.[24] For example, many hold that the solution to changes in the contemporary family can be answered by fathers' reasserting their primacy, by forcing their children and wives into blind obedience.[25] Or, they say, premarital sex can be prevented by promoting abstinence. One popular spokesman, Tim LaHaye, asserts that the antidote to sexual desire, especially on the part of teenagers, lies in censoring reading materials (see LaHaye 1980). Strict parental discipline automatically engenders self-discipline in children, he asserts.[26] The implication is that enforced other-directedness by parents produces inner-directed children, while the evidence indicates that they are more likely to exchange parental authoritarianism for that of another parental figure. To develop inner-direction under such circumstances requires, as a first step, rebellion against and rejection of parental authority—the opposite of parental intent.[27]

One aspect of fundamentalism, particularly the Protestant variety, is its insistence on the subservient role of women.[28] The wife is expected to be subject to the direction of her husband, children to their father. While Luker (1983) found that anti-abortionists in California supported this position and that proponents of choice generally favored equal status for women, recent research has shown that reasons for involvement in the anti-abortion movement vary by denomination. That is, some Catholics tend to be involved in the movement more from a "right to life" position, while Protestants and other Catholics are more concerned with sexual morality.[29] The broader right to life position is consistent with the official Catholic position against the death penalty and nuclear arms, while Protestant fundamentalists generally support the death penalty and a strong military.[30] Thus, Protestant fundamentalists, and some Catholic activists, appear to be more concerned with premarital sexual behavior than with the life of the fetus.[31]

Protestants and Catholics (especially traditional, ethnic Catholics), however, are both concerned with the "proper," or subordinate, role of women and the dominant role of men.[32] Wives should obey their husbands, and unmarried women should refrain from sexual intercourse. Abortion, for the Protestants in particular, is an indication of sexual licentiousness (see, for example, LaHaye 1980). Therefore, the total abolition of abortion would be a strong deterrent to such behavior, helping to reestablish traditional morality in women.[33] Contemporary, more liberal views of sexual morality cast the virgin female as deviant. The male virgin has long been regarded as deviant. The fundamentalist ethic appears to accept this traditional double standard with its relative silence on male virginity.

Another aspect of this gender role ethic lies in the home-related roles of females. Women are expected to remain at home, to bear children, and to care for them, while also serving the needs of their husbands. Again, this is also related to social class and the social role expectations of the lower and working classes, who tend to expect women to "stay in their place."

Luker's (1983) research reveals that some women in the anti-abortion movement are motivated by a concern for maintaining their ability to rely on men (husbands) to support their social roles as mothers,[34] while pro-choice women tend to want to maintain their independent status. Some of the men involved in anti-abortion violence are clearly acting out of a desire to maintain the dependent status of women and the dominant roles of men. Some of those violent males reveal an inability to establish "normal" relationships with women, which indicates that their violence may arise from a basic insecurity with the performance of normal male roles in relationships with women. This does not mean that these men do not have relationships with women. Indeed, it is in the context of relationships with women that dominance-related tendencies become more manifest. It is likely that insecurity-driven behaviors are characteristic of violent males generally, but psychiatric data are not available to confirm this, even for the population in question.[35]

The Complex of Fundamentalist Issues

The values and beliefs inherent to religious and cultural fundamentalism are expressed in a number of issues other than abortion. Those issues bear some discussion here, particularly as they relate to the abortion question.

1. *Contraception.* Fundamentalists, Catholic, Protestant, and Mormon, generally oppose the use of contraceptives since they limit family size and the intentions of God in sexuality.[36] They especially oppose sex education in the schools and the availability of contraceptives to minors without the approval of their parents. (See *Nightline*, 21 July 1989.) This is because control of women and sexuality are intertwined. If a girl has knowledge of birth control, she is potentially freed of the threat of pregnancy if she becomes sexually active. This frees her from parental control and discovery of illegitimate sexual intercourse.

2. *Prenatal testing, pregnancies from rape or incest, or those endangering a woman's life.* Since every pregnancy is divinely intended, opposition to prenatal testing arises from its use to abort severely defective fetuses and, in some cases, for sex selection.[37] Abortion is wrong regardless of the origins of the pregnancy or the consequences of it.

3. *In vitro fertilization, artificial fertilization, surrogate motherhood.* These are opposed because they interfere with the "natural" fertilization process and because they may mean the destruction of some fertilized embryos.

4. *Homosexuality.* Homophobia is characteristic of fundamentalism, because homosexual behavior is viewed as being "unnatural" and is prohibited in the Bible.[38]

5. *Uses of fetal tissue.* The use of fetal tissue in research and in the treatment of medical conditions such as Parkinson's disease is opposed, because it is thought to encourage abortion. (See *New York Times*, 16 August 1987; *Good Morning America*, 25 July 1991; *Face to Face with Connie Chung*, 25 November 1989; and *Nightline*, 6 January 1988.)

6. *Foreign relations issues.* Fundamentalists generally support aid to Israel and military funding (Diamond 1989). Indeed, as previously mentioned, they commonly view the United States as the New Israel. Protestant fundamentalists tend to be pre-millenialists, who maintain that biblical prophecies ordain that the reestablishment of the State of Israel will precede the Second Coming of Christ. Thus, they support aid to Israel to hasten the Second Coming, which actual-

ly, then, has an element of anti-Semitism to it, since Jews will not be among the saved.

7. *Euthanasia.* So-called right to life groups have frequently intervened in cases where relatives have sought to remove a patient from life-support systems. Most see a connection with abortion in that both abortion and the removal of life support interfere with God's decision as to when life should begin and end.

The most radical expression of cultural fundamentalism is that of Christian Reconstructionism,[39] to which Randall Terry, former director of Operation Rescue, subscribes. The adherents of Christian Reconstructionism, while a distinct minority, have some congregations of up to 12,000 members and count among their number Methodists, Presbyterians, Lutherans, Baptists, Catholics, and former Jews.[40] They are unabashed theocratists. They believe every area of life—law, politics, the arts, education, medicine, the media, business, and especially morality—should be governed in accordance with the tenets of Christian Reconstructionism. Some, such as Gary North, a prominent reconstructionist and son-in-law of Rousas John Rushdoony, considered the father of reconstructionism, would deny religious liberty—the freedom of religious expression—to "the enemies of God," whom the reconstructionists, of course, would identify.[41]

The reconstructionists want to establish a "God-centered government," a Kingdom of God on Earth, instituting the Old Testament as the Law of the Land. The goal of reconstructionism is to reestablish biblical, Jerusalemic society. Their program is quite specific. Those criminals which the Old Testament condemned to death would be executed, including homosexuals, sodomites, rapists, adulterers, and "incorrigible" youths. Jails would become primarily holding tanks for those awaiting execution or assignment as servants indentured to those whom they wronged as one form of restitution. The media would be censored extensively to reflect the views of the church. Public education and welfare would be abolished (only those who work should eat), and taxes would be limited to the tithe, 10 percent of income, regardless of income level, most of it paid to the church. Property, Social Security, and inheritance taxes would be eliminated. Church elders would serve as judges in courts overseeing moral issues, while "civil" courts would handle other issues. The country would return to the gold standard. Debts, including, for example, 30-

year mortgages, would be limited to 6 years. In short, Christian Reconstructionists see democracy as being opposed to Christianity, as placing the rule of man above the rule of God.[42] They also believe that "true" Christianity has its earthly rewards. They see it is the road to economic prosperity, with God blessing the faithful.

Chapter 5

Evolution of the Movement: From Polite to Fiery Protest

The character of the anti-abortion movement has changed over the years in terms of both the nature of its participants and its chosen forms of protest. This chapter examines that evolution, particularly in terms of the increasing incidence of anti-abortion-related violence and the effect on the movement of Ronald Reagan's first term as president.

The Conservative Character of Early Organizations

As stated earlier, the first anti-abortion organizations, galvanized in the 1960s in response to the campaigns to liberalize state abortion laws, tended to be small local groups of professionals, physicians, attorneys, and social workers who had contact with individuals caught in the abortion issue, such as social workers in adoption agencies or gynecologists-obstetricians, or who opposed the generally pro-abortion position of their professional associations (see Luker 1984). They were also largely Catholic. Most of the physicians probably practiced in Catholic hospitals, where anti-abortion attitudes and behaviors were taken for granted. They appear, from the descriptions given by Luker (1984), to have been isolated from those physicians in other types of practice who were coming into contact with the problems associated with illegal abortions or with more liberal abortion practices.[1]

Because these first organizations were composed primarily of professionals with ties to professional associations and other middle-class community organizations, the extent of their activism was limited; that is, their social positions and affiliations prevented them from appearing too strident or controversial and impelled them to participate in activities that could be interpreted as rational, reasonable, and polite. Their activities were designed to show the public that agreement with the reform/repeal movements was not universal and to awaken what they assumed was the "natural" public opposition to abortion to counteract liberalization.

As the number of states considering and enacting abortion liberalization laws increased, the anti-abortion movement began to move from the local to the national arena. Anti-abortion groups in various states began contacting their counterparts in other states, and a national network started to grow. One benchmark of the national movement was the establishment in 1967 of the Committee on Family Life by the National Catholic Bishops' Conference. After the 1973 *Roe v. Wade* and *Doe v. Bolton* Supreme Court rulings, national efforts intensified. One of the largest of the organizations formed at this time was the National Right to Life Committee (NRLC). It grew out of the Committee on Family Life of the National Catholic Bishops' Conference, but became independent and somewhat ecumenical. The NRLC was "traditional" in its methods and appeals; that is, it sought to counteract the Supreme Court's actions through lobbying and political pressure and to influence abortifacient producers through threatened boycotts. Its greatest efforts have been in lobbying for such laws as the human life amendment. The NRLC and similar anti-abortion organizations tend to be dominantly middle class in their orientation to effecting change.

Another coterie of opponents to abortion arose after the small groups of professionals began meeting in the 1960s. It was essentially composed of people who became active after reform or repeal was approved in their state and who became aware two or three years later of the extent of abortions being performed. These recruits formed new organizations and tended to have a social profile different from that of the members of the more moderate professional groups. They were largely lower-middle- and upper-working-class people who came to the movement primarily through religious networks (Himmelstein 1986). At this stage the Catholic source of recruitment began to be augmented by fundamentalist Protestants, primarily women, although men tended to be the leaders. These groups were more strident and activist in their opposition, while still concentrating on trying to reverse the new state laws.

The Turn to Radicalism

Public sentiment did not shift in support of the anti-abortion movement. While there have been ups and downs in public levels of approval and disapproval of abortion, since the early 1970s only about 15 percent of the population has approved a total ban on abortions. About 25 percent consistently approve abortion on demand, while the vast "middle" approve of abortion with some restrictions. More than 85 percent approve abortions in the cases of incest and rape. As one moves through the reasons for abortion, from the more drastic to the less drastic (such as being an unwed teenager down to not wanting the expense of another child), the support for abortion decreases. Yet the majority, approximately 75 percent, while not favoring abortion, still does not favor governmental restrictions. (See Gillespie 1988, Granberg 1978, McIntosh and Alston 1977, McIntosh *et al.* 1979.) It appears that this majority does not like the use of abortion as a form of birth control but would still leave the decision to the woman.

With the failure of lobbying and public education efforts, frustration set in and more radical and activist organizations began surfacing in the late 1970s and early 1980s. Examples of such organizations are John Ryan's St. Louis–based Pro-Life Direct Action League and Joseph Scheidler's Pro-Life Action League, currently the Pro-Life Action Network (PLAN). Anti-abortion "counseling" clinics sprang up across the nation, sponsored by groups like Birthright. They offer free pregnancy tests and then show videotapes and provide counseling designed to change a woman's mind about getting an abortion.

In the late 1970s other, even more activist, organizations arose that engaged in picketing clinics and physicians' offices and appealing to women entering them not to "kill" their babies. As the picketing alone seemed to have little effect, many groups became more hostile and more assertive. Epoxy cement was placed in clinic locks; stink bombs were ignited inside clinic bathrooms by bogus patients; bomb threats were called in to the clinics; clinic employees received threatening calls at home; patients were followed home or traced through license tags and loudly denounced in their own neighborhoods or before their families; judges conducting trials for anti-abortion activists who had violated the law were threatened; court trials of arsonists and bombers were picketed; some demonstrators carried preserved aborted fetuses; one clinic employee even found her beheaded cat on her doorstep; several clinic personnel were injured during incursions by protesters (Blanchard and Prewitt 1993).

A national network of these more activist individuals and groups arose, many connected through Joseph Scheidler's Pro-Life Action League (and later the Pro-Life Action Network). Groups in this category include Rescue America, Missionaries to the Preborn, and the Lambs of Christ. The active supporters of these groups appear to be dominantly working class and have a larger proportion of males than the more moderate professional groups.

Despite the efforts of such groups, the number of abortions performed remained fairly constant at about 1.5 million per year. Some activists began to initiate more violent acts. Table 1 delineates the rise and fall of the most serious types of violence against clinics and physicians.[2] Bombings and arsons did not begin until 1977, and there were 12 in the first two years. They then tapered off until there was a burst of renewed activity in 1984, which gradually declined to the present, but the rate is still higher than in the pre-1984 years.[3] The rate picked up again in 1991. Injuries resulting from violent acts include a clinic staff woman blown back into the street by an explosion just as she opened a clinic door; staff members in a Huntsville, Alabama, clinic injured by an ax-wielding priest; a clinic manager and the local NOW (National Organization for Women) president in a Pensacola, Florida, clinic injured when forcibly shoved by intruders; a physician and his wife kidnapped, held underground for eight days, and threatened with death; and a physician shot to death in 1993 in Pensacola (Blanchard and Prewitt 1993).

With the decline and leveling off of bombings and arsons, there arose several organizations whose activism lay between that of picketing and that of bombing; the best known of these is Operation Rescue. The militancy of Operation Rescue and related groups seized the headlines and has appeared to characterize, to the public, the anti-abortion movement from 1987—the date of Operation Rescue's founding—until the present. Table 2 indicates a broader view of more varied types of violence carried out by the anti-abortion movement through the years. Table 3 documents incidents considered disruptive. Hate mail and harassing calls, for example, were greatest in 1986 and 1991, while bomb threats peaked in 1985 and 1986, and picketing was modal in 1984–1986, 1988–1989, and 1991. Table 4 shows the number of clin-

TABLE 1

Frequency of Arsons and Bombings by Year, 1977–1992

Year	Number	Percent
1977	5	3.1
1978	7	4.3
1979	1	0.6
1980	0	0.0
1981	2	1.2
1982	7	4.3
1983	2	1.2
1984	30	18.6
1985	22	13.7
1986	14	8.7
1987	12	7.5
1988	7	4.3
1989	10	6.2
1990	8	5.0
1991	12	7.5
1992	22	13.7
TOTAL	161	99.9

SOURCE: National Abortion Federation.

ics blockaded, the number of blockades overall, and the numbers of arrests associated with those incidents; the heaviest blockade activity was in 1988–1989.

Thus, anti-abortion tactics have shifted over time. Picketing was the dominant tactic prior to 1984, while 1984 was the year for bombings, arsons, and attempted bombings and arsons, as well as for the beginning (1984–1986) of increased picketing, vandalism, invasions, and death threats.

A Rationale for Radicalism

I contend that there was a building frustration with the Reagan administration's lack of effectiveness in counteracting *Roe* and *Doe*. As the frustration grew, more activist elements came to the fore (see

TABLE 2
Frequency of Incidents of Violence and Disruption against Abortion Providers by Year

Type of Incident	1977–1983	1984	1985	1986	1987	1988	1989	1990	1991	Total
Bombing	8	18	4	2	0	0	2	0	0	34
Arson	13	6	8	7	4	4	6	4	8	60
Attempted bombing or arson	5	6	10	5	8	3	2	4	1	44
Invasion	68	34	47	53	14	6	25	19	25	291
Vandalism	35	35	49	43	29	29	24	25	40	309
Assault	11	7	7	11	5	5	12	6	5	69
Death threat	4	23	22	7	5	4	5	7	3	80
Kidnapping	2	0	0	0	0	0	0	0	0	2
Burglary	3	2	2	5	7	1	0	2	1	23
TOTAL	149	131	149	133	72	52	76	67	83	912

SOURCE: National Abortion Federation.

TABLE 3

Other Incidents of Disruption against Abortion Providers by Year

Type of Incident	1977–1983	1984	1985	1986	1987	1988	1989	1990	1991
Hate mail and harassing calls	9	17	32	53	32	19	30	21	99
Bomb threats	9	32	75	51	28	21	21	11	14
Picketing	107	160	139	141	77	151	151	45	275

SOURCE: National Abortion Federation.
NOTE: Numbers represent number of clinics as opposed to total incidents.

TABLE 4

Abortion Clinic Blockades, 1987–1991

Number	1987	1988	1989	1990	1991
Clinics	2	138	103	21	24
Incidents	2	182	201	34	29
Arrests	290	11,732	12,358	1,363	3,490

SOURCE: National Abortion Federation.

NOTE: Numbers are those reported by clinics to NAF. The number arrested represents multiple arrests for some persons.

Blanchard and Prewitt 1993). In sum, Reagan's apparent sympathy for the anti-abortion movement led to rising hopes for change, which were effectively dashed, the classic condition for an increase in violence.

Table 5 highlights the differences in the incidence of abortion-related violence between the Carter term and the first four years of Reagan's presidency. The more violent acts increased after the Reagan's first term and tapered off once he finally spoke out against anti-abortion violence in January 1985, after the almost simultaneous bombing of three clinics and offices in Pensacola, Florida, on Christmas morning 1984. Following that statement and the early 1985 arrests of a number of bombers and arsonists, the extreme violence decreased and milder forms of protest came to the fore (see Blanchard and Prewitt 1993). Picketing increased again 1988 and 1989, coinciding with the rise of Operation Rescue.

The 1993 murder of Dr. David Gunn in Pensacola and the shooting of Dr. George Tiller in Wichita, coupled with open statements by some movement activists supporting murder as a tactic, may indicate a rising level of frustration within the movement as a result of the 1992 election of Bill Clinton. Clinton's nullification of a number of Reagan-Bush limitations on federal support for abortion on the twentieth anniversary of *Roe v. Wade* and *Doe v. Bolton,* his pledge to sign the Freedom of Choice Act if it reaches his desk, and his effort to lift the ban on homosexuals in the military fly in the face of the movement's ideology and goals.

The majority of the most violent anti-abortionists, the arsonists and bombers, have been males, under 35 years of age, and rigid fundamentalists of Catholic, Protestant, or Mormon persuasion. Half had

TABLE 5

**Acts of Violence against Abortion Facilities,
1977–1980 and 1981–1984**

Type of Violence	1977–1980	1981–1984
Invasion	35	65
Vandalism	6	62
Death threat	1	25
Assault/battery	5	13
Burglary	0	5
Kidnaping/hostage taking	0	2
Attempted arson/bombing	2	9
Arson	8	11
Bombing	4	25
TOTAL	61	273

SOURCE: National Abortion Federation.

never been involved in previous anti-abortion activities. In particular, the vast majority were working class and had jobs in which they were self-employed or had a lot of discretionary time that gave them both opportunity for such actions and a "cover" for the preparatory activities. They also were *encapsulated,* having no significant social ties to groups outside those which would reinforce their worldview.[4] (See Blanchard and Prewitt 1993.)

In examining recruitment processes in the civil rights movement, McAdam argues for "the importance of both structural and individual motivational factors in high risk/cost activism." He adds that "an intense ideological identification with the values of the movement disposes the individual toward participation, while a prior history of activism and integration into supportive networks acts as a structural 'pull' encouraging the individual to make good on his or her strongly held beliefs" (1986:64). Thus, initial involvement in virtually any organization in a movement establishes relationships in a new network, which may well lead to additional involvements at other movement levels and in other activities.

A survey of the literature on the various anti-abortion movement organizations and the documents published by them suggests, I hypothesize, that in moving from the "mildest" organizations to the more extremist ones[5]:

1. The constituencies are less supportive of the broad "pro-life" position; i.e., the more exclusively anti-abortion the organizations tend to become.

2. The greater the importance of religious networks in organizational recruitment, especially the non-Catholic networks.

3. The more religiously fundamentalist the membership becomes, regardless of denomination.

4. The more Protestant vis-à-vis Catholic the organizations become.

5. The greater the emphasis on cultural fundamentalism.

6. The greater the dominance of males in the organizations.

7. The more adept the organizations become in tactics of collusion and deception; i.e., the more skilled at avoiding the consequences of civil suits and criminal penalties.

In chapters 6 and 7 we will look more closely at the nature of the organizations within the anti-abortion movement and at the strategies they have used in trying to attain their goals.

Chapter 6

The Organizations: Their Identities, Sources of Support, and Interactions

This chapter focuses on the anti-abortion organizations themselves, offering a history and description of the activities of the primary groups active today. It also discusses organizations' major resources: money, political support, and one another; one of the more interesting aspects of the anti-abortion movement is the way it has succeeded in bringing together extremely diverse groups, from traditional Catholics to Protestant fundamentalists to Mormons and, to a degree, from the nonviolent to the violent. Finally, and related to the idea of connection among the various groups that make up the movement, the chapter looks at the anti-abortion movement as an industry, with the older, larger, more traditional organizations functioning alongside spin-offs and start-ups.

The Major Anti-Abortion Organizations

While I have mentioned a number of the organizations in the anti-abortion movement, it is useful at this point to review in detail the major players.

The National Conference of Catholic Bishops' Committee for Pro-Life Activities   This is "the broadest, best organized and most powerful group, people on both sides of the issue say" (*New York Times*, 14 June 1992). Its basic functions include providing education and information to the public and assistance to diocesan and parish committees. In April 1990, the Bishops' Conference employed public relations firm Hill and Knowlton to conduct a five-year, $5 million campaign to educate the American public on the immorality of abortion.

The National Right to Life Committee   This group claimed 7 million members in 1992, more than any other organization in the movement (*New York Times,* 14 June 1992). Established by the Catholic Church, it is currently ecumenical, but still predominantly Catholic in membership and funding sources. It stresses lobbying and education, while opposing violence and the methods typical of groups like Operation Rescue.

In 1980 the NRLC had an annual budget of $1.3 million, five full-time and four part-time staff, and a membership of 11 million (Margolis 1980). By 1985 its budget was $4.5 million, and the National Right to Life Political Action Committee had a $750,000 budget, more than double its 1982 budget of $300,000 (Cuniberti and Mehren 1985). In its fiscal year ending 30 April 1988, the NRLC reported an income of $6.5 million, with 31 percent of that spent on programs. Its lobbying efforts include support for the human life amendment, which would add to the Constitution a provision declaring the personhood of the fetus from the moment of conception.[1] It also uses lawsuits to discourage doctors from performing abortions, pressures insurance companies not to insure physicians who perform abortions, works to get states to deny public funds and use of public hospitals for abortions, and pressures drug companies not to produce abortifacients (Caplan 1989). It has sponsored a long-standing boycott against the Upjohn Company for its production of Prostin F2a, used to end second-trimester pregnancies. The Christian Action Council, a Protestant group, also supports the boycott.

With its broad appeal through traditional church hierarchical channels and its more "acceptable" activities, such as lobbying, the NRLC appears to have the broadest support among the population at large of any organization in the anti-abortion movement. It also has subsidiary organizations in every state and virtually every major metropolitan area in the country. Its successes have been limited, however. It scored a success with the abrogation of federal funding for abortions through Medicaid and in military hospitals, but it has failed to get the human life amendment passed by Congress.

The NRLC, relatively well-funded through a broad membership and regular monies from churches, has a stable national staff in Washington, D.C., and professional lobbyists. It makes few personal demands on its membership beyond writing letters and such. Its primary work is done by a professional staff who can use the weight of their membership size when lobbying or testifying before congressional committees and through its state and local affiliates. The NRLC and anti-abortion organizations like it thus tend to take a conservative, typically "middle-class" approach to effecting change.

The NRLC and other anti-abortion lobbyists have been effective in getting more restrictive laws passed in a number of states and carrying them through the appeal process toward pressuring the Supreme Court to limit the effects of, and to eventually overturn, *Roe v. Wade* and *Doe v. Bolton*. The *Webster* decision in 1989, which opened the door for states to place some restrictions on abortions, marks its greatest success to date. Other successes have been in the administration and congressional limitations on the use of federal funds for abortions and abortion counseling.

The American Life League   This group is a spin-off of the NRLC, with a more activist orientation. With 250,000 members, it supports "nonviolent direct action, sidewalk counseling, post-abortion counseling and adoption referrals" (Caplan 1989). Judie and Paul Brown, with the fund-raising help of Paul Weyrich, a major tactician in the Reagan elections of 1980 and 1984, founded the organization to move closer to the New Right and a more activist religious stance (*Economist*, 5 August 1989). It is also opposed to birth control and has supported, in opposition to the NRLC, the activities of Operation Rescue and similar groups. Its 1990 budget was $8.2 million.

The Pro-Life Nonviolent Action Project   Founded by John Cavanaugh-O'Keefe, this group is headquartered in Gaithersburg, Maryland. O'Keefe is regarded as the father of the more activist wing of the movement. He began organizing "peaceful presence" sit-ins in 1975.

Feminists for Life   Feminists for Life claimed 1500 members in 1987 (Gallagher 1987). The group maintains a hotline and a newsletter, *Sisterlife*, and runs occasional ads supporting women who bear to term.

Pro-Lifers for Survival   Founded by Juli Loesch (now Loesch Wiley), this group grew out of the anti-nuclear arms movement and continues to connect the two issues.

Women Exploited by Abortion   This is another organization in the right-wing coalition (*Economist*, 5 August 1989). It is composed of women who have had abortions and later regretted it. They concentrate on letter campaigns and similar activities. Their primary theme is "post-abortion depression" or "the post-abortion syndrome." The majority of the objective research, however, indicates that this is a problem for a very small minority of women who have abortions. While some anti-abortion activists claim that as many as 90 percent of the women getting abortions undergo such depression, the research indicates that it is closer to 1 percent (Planned Parenthood 1991). Some evidence indicates that there is a much greater incidence of depression occurring among women who bear to term and give up their infants to adoption (Planned Parenthood 1991). Diamond (1989:98) contends that the "post-abortion syndrome" experienced by WEBA members is likely a guilt trip instigated by the condemnations of TV evangelists and their fundamentalist pastors.

Victims of Choice   This organization is similar to WEBA.

Concerned Women for America   Beverly LaHaye founded this organization in 1979 to activate women on a broad range of political issues, including abortion. It has local chapters in communities across the country and has been able to mobilize and inspire women across a number of fundamentalist and evangelical denominations. In 1987 its budget was reported to be $6 million (Brozan 1987, cited in Diamond 1989).

Operation Rescue   Operation Rescue practices primarily clinic blockades. Its membership is dominantly Protestant fundamentalists. According to Suh (1989:92), Operation Rescue was organized in 1986 by Randall Terry with the help of Joseph Scheidler. Some maintain that it became a "front" for Scheidler following the several civil suits against him (see also Tumulty and Smith 1989 and Faux 1990), while others see conflict in recent years between Terry and Scheidler. Also, Terry served on the board of Scheidler's Pro-Life Action League when he conceived of Operation Rescue and first proposed that type of action to the league before forming Operation Rescue.

The first major clinic blockades by Operation Rescue took place in 1987 in Cherry Hill, Pennsylvania (Maxwell 1992). "From the end of October to mid-February [1988–89], there has been at least one locally organized Operation Rescue act every weekend. There have been at least 130 protests altogether in 35 states, and some 12,000 arrests" (Suh 1989:92). The resulting publicity helped Operation Rescue's budget grow from $43,000 in 1987 to $300,000 in 1988 (Suh 1989:93). While it appears to have only about 300 "hard-core" members, it has "sympathizers in about 100 affiliated groups nationwide (Smith 1989).[2] The group's objectives, according to Cal Thomas, a syndicated newspaper columnist sympathetic to Operation Rescue (1988), are primarily to (1) prevent all abortions on the day of demonstrations, (2) close other clinics that day because of higher tension and a sense of threat, (3) put the broader pro-choice groups on the defensive, and (4) add momentum to the "pro-life" movement. Operation Rescue leaders are particularly skilled in orchestrating demonstrations. They usually meet a day or two before a "rescue" with law enforcement officials and explain their plan of action, down to the timetable for events, the number of people designated to attempt to break through police lines, and way those people will behave while undergoing arrest.[3]

As head of Operation Rescue, Terry eventually put all contributions into his personal checking account to frustrate judgments against the group. Once the suits from clinics and pro-choice organizations increased, he relinquished control of Operation Rescue and closed the Binghamton, New York, office in 1990, when fines against the group totaled $475,000. He then established a new organization, REAP, to sell materials and supplies. In 1992, Pat Mahoney closed the Florida office because of heavy fines. The Rev. Kenneth Tucci then assumed leadership and established headquarters in Summerville, South Carolina. As of summer 1993 the group still maintained a training camp for protesters in Melbourne, Florida, using local clinics for training.

Operation Rescue leaders appear to be related to 30 or more churches scattered across the country in their principle organizational cities. Some observers of the organization maintain that these "shadow" churches were perhaps organized primarily as front organizations for "washing" contributions to keep them from being seized by various courts, much as organized crime uses legitimate businesses to launder illegally gained profits. Other organizations, such as the Committee to Protect the Family Foundation, began collecting funds for Operation Rescue's use (Pratt n.d.). Terry also organized the American Anti-Persecution League in 1992 to "sue anyone who violates a pro-life demonstrator's civil rights."

In 1991 Operation Rescue began using children in its blockades in Wichita, Baton Rouge, and elsewhere in an effort to cast the police in a negative light for arresting children. Some courts responded by citing the children for delinquency and the parents for contributing to the delinquency of minors. Operation Rescue has also been accused of using fake clinic clients to testify that one of its events had led them to decide against abortion. By 1992 injunctions or fines had been exacted in Oregon, California, Massachusetts, Florida, Pennsylvania, and New York. Operation Rescue was under siege from court suits, especially under RICO (Racketeer Influenced Corrupt Organizations) laws,[4] and from an accumulation of fines amounting well into six figures.[5] Attempts to seize the group's assets have been minimally successful, since Terry never filed for tax-exempt status and deposited all donations in personal accounts (Dionne 1989b and Tumulty and Smith 1989). It also appears that new organizations were created to "replace" the group and to handle its funds.

Despite the Supreme Court ruling that the Ku Klux Klan law, which made actions against classes of persons (such as racial category) illegal, did not apply to abortion protests, a Washington, D.C., federal judge determined in March 1993 that a fine of $282,610 could still be enforced against Operation Rescue and three leaders on the basis of district trespassing and public nuisance laws. The fines were to be paid to the clinics the protesters had targeted (*Dallas Morning News,* 17 March 1993).

The tactics of Operation Rescue and similar groups, such as Scheidler's, have had an impact on the availability of abortion. While 84 percent of the members of the American College of Obstetricians and Gynecologists have said they think "abortion should be legal and available," only about a third of those approving perform them, and two-thirds of those performing them said they performed very few. Those physicians who do perform abortions feel that they are stigmatized (Kolata 1990:1). Only 17 percent of U.S. counties appear to have abortions available, and those physicians performing abortions in clinics seem to come from somewhat distant communities to avoid local stigmatization.

In 1989, the New Jersey Catholic Bishops organization issued a statement giving strong support to Operation Rescue (Planned Parenthood 1989). On 15 November 1991, the Pope met with Randall Terry at the Vatican during the course of a meeting with 150 representatives of eight anti-abortion groups (Kissling 1991:21). The attendees petitioned the Pope to excommunicate pro-choice Catholic politicians and other outspoken pro-choice Catholics. The Pope's reception of Terry among the others gave an air of legitimacy to Operation Rescue and its methods.

Operation Rescue has conducted clinic blockades, the most notorious being in Atlanta during the 1988 Democratic Party Convention and in 1991 in Wichita. Terry has made it clear that his ultimate goals deal with more than the abortion issue. Indeed, his goals are close to those of the Christian Reconstructionists. He claims to be inspired by the works of Francis Schaeffer, who decried the loss of the absolutist early Reformation and the rise of the Renaissance and called for fundamentalist political action (Faux 1990).

Life Dynamics   Located in Lewisville, Texas, Life Dynamics is headed by Mark Crutcher, a former activist in the Operation Rescue organization in Texas. He has developed a seminar for "life activists" on establishing deceptive "crisis" centers. He has also authored a book, *Firestorm: A Guerrilla Strategy for a Pro-Life America*, in which he argues that trying to get abortion criminalized again is futile and that the best hope lies in harassing abortion providers to the point that they quit, thereby making abortions unavailable.

He has mailed out a list of clinics' and physicians' 800 telephone numbers with instructions on how to tie up their phone lines and increase their costs through multiple calls. He has also mailed out a deceptive survey to abortion providers to determine the effects of harassment. In August 1993 he began assembling a national data file on all physicians performing abortions, with information on the clinics and hospitals where they performed them. The stated purpose of the file was to assist attorneys suing abortion providers for malpractice.

The Arthur DeMoss Foundation   This group has ties to Senator Jesse Helms and Jerry Falwell (Kissling 1991). It gives funds to several anti-abortion organizations and in 1992 began sponsoring a broad television media campaign urging women to carry their pregnancy to term. The campaign theme, "Life. What a beautiful choice," was turned by pro-choicers into "Choice. What a beautiful life."

Birthright Birthright, founded in 1968 in Toronto, runs about 500 pregnancy counseling centers in the United States, as well as a number in other countries. It is reputedly financed largely by the Pearson Foundation.[6] The foundation was established by Robert Pearson, the primary organizer of the opposition to the Hawaii movement to repeal that state's abortion laws. These clinics have been widely criticized for their deceptive tactics: volunteers wearing white jackets resembling those of physicians; advertising themselves as abortion clinics; implying in their names, ads, and over the telephone that they perform abortions; locating themselves near a real clinic to confuse those going to it (Berger 1986, Uehling 1986, Wong 1987).

Congressional and other investigations indicate that there are as many as 3,000 of these clinics, not all, of course, related to Birthright. When these types of clinics began operating in the late 1970s and early 1980s, they frequently advertised in the yellow pages of telephone books under the heading "Abortion Services" and under similar deceptive rubrics in newspaper classified ads. Rising complaints and threatened court suits from abortion providers have led to new listings, such as "Abortion Alternatives," separate from "Abortion Services." The "Abortion Alternatives" heading carries a note: "Organizations Listed At This Heading Provide Free Assistance, Counseling And/Or Information On Abortion Alternatives. They Do Not Provide Abortion Services Or Counseling Or Information On The Attainment Of Abortion Or Birth Control Services."

On 26 October 1992 a San Diego Planned Parenthood chapter filed a suit against four such clinics in the San Diego area, charging them with false advertising and consumer fraud (*Pensacola News Journal*, 27 October 1992). In 1986 the Problem Pregnancy Center in Fort Worth was convicted of violating the Texas Deceptive Trade Practices Act and ordered to pay $39,000 in fines and $69,000 in attorneys' fees.

Human Life International This group is headed by the Rev. Paul Marx, O.S.B., out of Gaithersburg, Maryland, the site of a number of clinic bombings and arsons. It claims 25,000 members in at least 30 countries. Primarily Catholic, it supports Operation Rescue–type activities in Africa and Asia (*Pensacola News Journal*, 27 October 1992).[7] A Catholic priest, Marx is the author of *The Death Peddlers: War on the Unborn*. He established the Human Life Center in 1972 and Human Life International in 1981.

The Pro-Life Action League   The Pro-Life Action League (PLAL), organized by Joseph Scheidler in 1980 and later expanded to include the organization the Pro-Life Action Network (PLAN), operates out of Chicago. Scheidler's original board consisted of himself, his wife, and his secretary. Described by Patrick Buchanan as "the green beret of the prolife movement" (Vinzant 1993), he is a former Benedictine monk and author of *Closed: 99 Ways to Stop Abortion* (1985). Scheidler formerly worked for the Illinois Right to Life Committee and for Friends for Life, but was fired from the former and asked to resign from the latter because of his activism. In addition to abortion, Scheidler opposes birth control as "disgusting, just mutual masturbation" as well as sex education in schools (Schwartz 1985). Scheidler stages Operation Rescue–type demonstrations and cooperates with Operation Rescue. According to some, he fostered the organization of Operation Rescue to avoid more court suits from clinics and pro-choice organizations. Scheidler is a central figure in keeping elements of the activist wing informed about one another. His tactics have been adopted and elaborated on by other organizations, such as Missionaries to the Pre-Born, Rescue America, and the Lambs of Christ.

Scheidler is virtually a father figure among activists. His book advises anti-abortion groups to adopt more dramatic tactics, such as picketing physicians' homes and embarrassing them in public places, such as airports, with demonstrations. While explicitly disavowing violence and other illegal activities, his book describes a number of those tactics well enough to offer basic guidelines to those who might adopt them. Furthermore, he keeps in touch with and visits those sentenced to prison for such acts as bombings and arsons, attends some of their trials, and has even presented some of the these activists with awards. Some bombers and arsonists claim to have received their inspirations while attending a Scheidler event (Blanchard and Prewitt 1993).

John Brockhoeft, convicted of conspiracy to bomb a Pensacola clinic in 1988 and of bombing at least one in Cincinnati in 1990, met another activist, John Burt, at a Scheidler meeting. He later drove with a bomb in his trunk from Kentucky to Pensacola, where John Burt showed him the location of the Ladies Center. Scheidler was present at the demonstration during which John Burt and Joan Andrews invaded the Pensacola Ladies Center and on the prior evening was the key speaker at a rally for the next day's events. Randall Terry was a member of Scheidler's board and first proposed "rescues" to that group before organizing Operation Rescue, which follows many of the more radical suggestions in Scheidler's book. Scheidler also began a "litigation project" that assists in filing suits against clinics (Diamond 1989:90).

Pro-Life Direct Action League   The PDAL is primarily a St. Louis, Missouri, organization initiated and directed by John Ryan, who conducted sit-ins there virtually alone for a year. After three years, PDAL virtually dissolved when Ryan was discovered to be having an affair with a woman in the organization.[8]

Lambs of Christ   Lambs of Christ was formed in 1988 under the name of Victim Souls of the Unborn Christ Child by Father Norman Weslin, a priest of the Oblates of Wisdom order. It reportedly has 30–40 full-time members prepared to travel primarily through the Midwest for Operation Rescue sorts of demonstrations in which the object is to enter clinics or blockade them. The group has about 250 part-time members and around 3,000 others who support the activists through prayer, occasional housing for demonstrations, and money. Weslin is a retired U.S. Army colonel, and his organization is structured along paramilitary lines (*Time*, 4 May 1992).

On arrest, the Lambs refuse to give their names to the police or jailers, instead adopting pseudonyms similar to Weslin's "Baby John Doe." Prior to demonstrations, they reportedly take laxatives and on arrest defecate on themselves (personal interview with observers and law enforcement personnel). Once sentenced to jail terms, the Lambs have been more effective in maintaining their commitment than many other groups. They continue to conduct passive resistance there, while conducting regular masses and other rites of mutual support.[9]

Missionaries to the Pre-Born   This group was established by an Assembly of God minister, Matthew Trewhella. Another primary figure is Joe Foreman, a one-time Presbyterian minister and former activist in Operation Rescue who kept up on Operation Rescue members in jails. The Missionaries are a Protestant counterpart to the Lambs, and, like the Lambs, have a core of virtually full-time activists, number 45 as of 1992 (Maxwell 1992). Foreman's radio broadcasts in the Milwaukee area are inflammatory; he has, for instance, compared physicians who perform abortions to India's man-eating tigers, which have to be killed.

Rescue America   Operating out of Houston and headed by Donald Treshman, Rescue America follows the tactics of Operation Rescue. Treshman's hotline celebrated the torching of a Beaumont, Texas, clinic and "gave a detailed how-to description for those of like mind" (Planned Parenthood 1992b). Treshman was convicted by a Texas court of trespassing as head of Texas Life Advocates, another anti-abortion organization, for distributing leaflets at a high school without permission and refusing to leave. He was sentenced to 104 days in prison and a $1000 fine (Planned Parenthood 1991).

Treshman, a Presbyterian minister, established Rescue America as Houston Rescue in 1986, but the organization soon became national. Dr. David Gunn was killed at a Pensacola, Florida, clinic in March 1993 during a demonstration led by Rescue America, and his killer had participated in several of their previous demonstrations *(Macon Telegraph* 1993). Rescue America cooperated with Operation Rescue in the demonstrations at the Republican party convention in Houston in 1992. An affiliate, Dallas Pro Life Action Network, was sued in 1993 by an obstetrician for stalking and harassing him and his wife.

In all the activities of the anti-abortion movement organizations, it is clear that impact on the public and on politicians is not necessarily related to the size of the organization. The more radical the activity of the organization, the more likely it is to receive significant attention from the press. Very small groups of bombers have received greater attention, for the most part, than has the NRLC, the largest organization in the movement. The same is true of the quite small Lambs of Christ and Missionaries to the Pre-Born. It is a lesson well learned by a number of activists, such as John Burt (the leader of the Pensacola activists since 1982) with his use of Baby Charlie, a preserved fetus, and Randall Terry.

Black Americans for Life   This group was organized in 1986 and claimed more than 3,000 members in 1987. Its president at that time, Kay James, had worked previously for the NRLC. It is a subgroup of the NRLC (*Christianity Today*, 2 October 1987).

JustLife   JustLife was formed in 1986 by a coalition of Catholics and Protestants as a political action committee to endorse anti-abortion candidates. Other issues on their platform include opposition to nuclear weapons and justice for the poor (*Christianity Today,* 13 June 1986).

Last Days Ministries   Melody Green, head of a Christian commune, Last Days Ministries, in Lindale, Texas, was one of the early users of preserved fetuses in demonstrations. She typically issues a call for followers to "fight in God's Army" (Diamond 94).

Americans United for Life   This group is the major legal arm of the movement, designed to provide attorneys for organizations and individuals under criminal or civil suits.

Sources of Support

Resources important to the movement have been diverse. One, of course, is money. While initial and continuing basic financial support has come through Catholic sources, from the Catholic Bishops' Conference, from virtually every diocese and numberless parishes, most of that money flows to organizations dominated by Catholics, particularly the National Right to Life Committee and others devoted to traditional, "civil" political action.

In the early 1980s, the Protestant elements of the movement began to tap into right-wing funding sources, foundations, and individuals, particularly through the contacts and support of Paul Weyrich and Richard Viguerie, a master strategist for the right wing who had worked on George Wallace's presidential campaigns. Christian television networks and stations also provided avenues for tapping large numbers of small donations for those using that medium, such as Weyrich's American Life League.

An important resource of the movement has been political access. The first major political response to the 1973 Supreme Court decisions was the 1976 passage of the Hyde Amendment, which barred the use of federal Medicaid dollars for abortion unless the mother's life was in danger. In the same year the equal rights amendment died, which had two effects: it was viewed as a victory for the traditionalists, and it freed those who had been fighting it to pick up another issue—abortion. In other words, mobilization against the ERA provided organizations ready-made to attack something else.

In the same year the human life amendment was introduced, giving the anti-abortion movement additional hope that *Roe* and *Doe* could be overturned. The amendment would ban abortions except to save the woman's life. Another amendment offered would have banned all abortions, without exceptions, while still another would have allowed the states to establish their own policies.

Meanwhile, the election of Jimmy Carter as president was another hopeful sign. While in some congressional districts, especially in the South, evangelicals have felt a sense of power in being able to elect representatives who appeared to represent their views, their first sense of representation in the White House in this century came with the election of Carter, a professed born-again Christian. The election gave a number of evangelicals their first taste of political organizing and probably initiated the largest number of interorganizational contacts and coalition formations since prohibition. This is noteworthy, for many evangelicals probably felt shut out of the circles of power during the New Deal and subsequent administrations, especially during the civil rights era. The successful election of Carter gave many a renewed sense of efficacy.

While Carter gave anti-abortion movement supporters a minor success when he cut off of Medicaid funds for abortions by signing a bill with the Hyde Amendment attached,[10] a real sense of empowerment came with Ronald Reagan's election. In acts of symbolic or rhetorical support, Reagan wrote an article against abortion for the *Human Life Review*, published by Human Life International (Reagan 1983); spoke to the March for Life annually by telephone, a practice followed by George Bush (Clendinen 1985); gave major addresses to anti-abortion organizations; and, as mentioned in chapter 3, entertained anti-abortion leaders in the White House, including Joseph Scheidler (Toner 1986, May 1986). Reagan of course also implemented policies related to the abortion issue, including the ban on the use of fetal tissue in research and in the treatment of illnesses such as Parkinson's disease, on the grounds that these activities might encourage abortion; and the ban on the U.S. importation of RU-486, the so-called abortion pill that a French corporation began distributing in 1985. RU-486 is successful in inducing miscarriage during the first trimester of pregnancy (Whitney 1991).[11] While swallowing a pill is "easier" than a having a traditional abortion, ingestion of RU-486 does require the supervision of a physician and has about the same cost as an abortion. The controversy revolves around its use as an abortifacient.

Reagan also refused to define abortion clinic bombings and arsons as terrorism, which kept them out of the hands of the Federal Bureau of Investigation and under the auspices of the Bureau of Alcohol, Tobacco, and Firearms.[12] Paul Brown of the American Life League and Joseph Scheidler reportedly asked Reagan to pardon those abortion clinic bombers and arsonists in prison. Reportedly, Reagan pledged to review their standing on a case-by-case basis (May 1986), but he ultimately did not pardon any of those so convicted. He further angered clinics and abortion providers by not condemning bombings and arsons, despite their frequent urgings, until January 1985.

The most startling charge regarding the Reagan administration was made by Carl Bernstein in 1992 (Bernstein 1992). Bernstein maintains, based on several administration sources, that Reagan struck a deal with Pope John Paul II in 1982 that involved the Vatican's funnelling U.S. funds to the Polish Solidarity organization in exchange for the administration's cutting off funds for birth control and abortion internationally. Reagan cut off funding to the International Planned Parenthood Federation and the United Nations Fund for Population Activities in 1984.

George Bush's presidency largely maintained Reagan's policies, including the ban on fetal tissue research and RU-486. As discussed in chapter 3, he amended the ban on abortion counseling at facilities receiving federal funds. The primary organization affected by this regulation was Planned Parenthood, which contested the decision in the courts on the grounds that it interfered with the physician-patient relationship. The administration compromised in 1992 by limiting the regulation to nonphysicians (Hilts 1991). When the restrictions went into effect in October 1992, some Planned Parenthood offices rejected federal funds rather than submit, while others practiced, in effect, civil disobedience by ignoring the regulations (Hall 1992b).[13] It appears that those organizations depending on federal sources for the majority of their support tended to take the latter course. On election day, 3 November 1992, it was announced that a federal appeals court had ruled that President Bush's directive was illegal since the law required public hearings before changing a federal regulation or instituting a new one.

In another development, the Justice Department intervened in Wichita, Kansas, on behalf of demonstrators for Operation Rescue. In 1991 Operation Rescue staged a demonstration for several weeks in Wichita. Federal Judge Patrick Kelly ordered federal marshals to protect women entering abortion clinics and levied fines and issued injunctions against the demonstrators, which resulted in the jailing of a number of them. The Justice Department filed briefs opposing the injunctions and jailings, maintaining that clinic blockades constituted freedom of speech under the Fifth Amendment. Kelly's rulings were upheld by an appeals court.

Bush also vetoed a bill in 1992 that would have allowed the use of Medicaid funds for abortion for victims of incest or rape, and, as noted previously, he vetoed the freedom of choice bill, which would have made the provisions of *Roe* and *Doe* statutory law; Congress's attempt to override the veto failed.

Another primary political source of support for the anti-abortion movement in the 1980s was the Moral Majority. Under the stewardship of Vigurie and Weyrich, Jerry Falwell, pastor of Liberty Baptist Church and head of Liberty College in Lynchburg, Virginia, founded the Moral Majority in 1979, as Ronald Reagan was beginning his campaign for the Republican nomination, to counteract the "liberalizing" tendencies in American society.[14] Abortion was only one item in its catalog of American sins. The Moral Majority supported Ronald Reagan and George Bush in their elections, as well as a host of state and local candidates who supported its agenda. It also targeted for defeat candidates for both houses of Congress who supported abortion or disagreed with other items on its agenda. Falwell had organizations in every state and in most metropolitan communities to lobby, boycott, and picket on local issues, such as the sale of *Playboy* in convenience stores and the teaching of evolution instead of creationism in public schools.

The Moral Majority was given widespread media coverage, especially just before and after the first Reagan election, with both reporters and Falwellians appearing to assume that it had a decisive effect on the election. Subsequent studies have concluded that it had little, if any, effect on the election itself. Even those who supported the stances of the Moral Majority did not vote on that basis. The evidence is that most Americans voted in 1980, 1984, and 1988 on economic rather than "moral" issues (see Bromley and Shupe 1984, Bruce 1990, Ferguson and Rogers 1986, Himmelstein and McRae 1984, and Liebman and Wuthnow 1983). The Moral Majority was disbanded in 1990.

Presidential support for the movement may be related to the unwillingness of the more moderate anti-abortion organizations to completely distance themselves from the most violent.[15] In many social movements, "moderate social movement organizations (SMOs) often denounce radical SMOs for statements and actions that threaten to alienate potential sources of external support" (Barkan 1986:190); this has seldom happened in the case of the anti-abortion movement. The Catholic Bishops' Conference blamed bombings on the existence of the clinics, as did others perceived as moderates, such as John Willke, leader of the Right to Life Committee.

The conservative Court majority created by Bush and Reagan that weighed in on the *Webster* decision, combined with the presidential actions cited above, gave new impetus to anti-abortion efforts at the state level by the end of the 1980s. By January 1992, for example, a total of 40 states had passed or retained parental consent laws, 15 of them enforcing these laws. At the same time, only 13 states allowed the use of Medicaid funds for abortions.

The major impact of four consecutive presidential terms supporting aspects of the anti-abortion movement, however, probably lies in having given the activists, a very small minority of the American population, an aura of legitimacy. This in turn may have contributed to the hesitancy of law enforcement officials across the nation in moving decisively against Operation Rescue–type activists. The combination of "stand-by" law enforcement and tacit presidential endorsement led to virtually continual media attention, which kept the issue before the public and made the movement appear stronger than it was. These factors alone would have made it easier for the movement to recruit additional adherents. Furthermore, this sense of gaining momentum would tend to lead to an escalating degree of activism and radical action.

Another source of support for the anti-abortion movement amounts to what might be called organizational endorsements. As the movement in general became more vocal, organized, and active, groups that had initially endorsed *Roe* and *Doe* began to reassess their positions, some even reversing their original endorsement and others tempering theirs. One particular public segment, religious bodies, underwent a shift. While individuals are not likely to be heavily influenced by official denominational pronouncements,[16] the cumulative effect of major denomination after denomination tempering and backtracking perhaps had the effect of encouraging individuals to reassess their own positions and to begin to look at greater depth into the nuances of the abortion decision. While the percentage of public support for unfettered choice declined a little, as did the complete opposition to it, the "middle ground" grew as people appeared to become more discriminating about the conditions under which they would consider abortion to be acceptable. While I have found no research connecting changing organizational stances to the perceived change on the part of the general public, the effect may have been to lessen the approval of unlimited access to abortion. Certainly, when the largest Protestant denomination, the Southern Baptist Convention, came out against abortion, it helped cast an atmosphere of greater legitimacy over the anti-abortion movement. It was no longer just a Catholic versus Protestant issue.

In the late 1970s and early 1980s what appears to be a strange phenomenon occurred. Suddenly, there were Catholics, Protestant fundamentalists, Mormons, and even a few mainline Protestants and Mormons working together in various organizations and demonstrations.[17] Groups that would ordinarily ignore, if not castigate, one another, were working side by side: Catholics, Mormons, charismatics, anti-charismatics.

Divisions, Linkages, Coalitions, and Start-Ups: The Creation of an Industry

The major national anti-abortion organization, the National Right to Life Committee, was originated primarily by Catholics. It has since managed to garner support from Protestant and other non-Catholic groups and individuals. As stated above, it remains the largest anti-abortion movement organization. This is probably because of its broad appeal, based on its concentration on education and lobbying, as well as its relatively secure funding, which allows it to file opinions in court cases, publish newsletters, and engage in other activities that keep it before the public eye.

It has suffered divisions, however. Judie Brown left it to form the American Life League because she felt it was not activist enough. John Willke, its chief executive for a long period, left in 1991 because he approved of abortion in cases of rape and incest.[18] Such splits and "theological," ideological, and tactical disputes are a normal part of the process of social movement development. Adaptation and organizational change tend to be slow, however, exacerbating the likelihood of developing movement "sects."[19]

While such splits may affect individual organizations negatively, reducing their financial and membership resources, this mitosis of movement organizations is not necessarily detrimental to the movement. Indeed, it may well facilitate movement growth and development. That is, new organizations with new tactics and emphases will probably bring new constituencies into a degree of participation in the movement, helping it to expand and increase its power.[20] Furthermore, the development of new groups with new tactics and strategies, and even goals, may help to further change the external environment and eventually force the original organization to adapt and change its tactics and goals. In addition, such splits may help organizations focus their efforts more clearly and eventually lead to even greater resource development.

While an organization such as the NRLC may at first decry those who leave it to form new organizations, as a movement develops and increasingly radical groups arise, accommodations will be made, especially for those who are closest in goals, tactics, and strategies. For example, while the NRLC and the majority of anti-abortion movement organizations eschew and condemn the use of violence, most tacitly endorsed the bombings and arsons. A justification for the bombings and arsons came from none other than the Roman Catholic bishops of the United States when in January 1985 they condemned the spate of bombings as a symptom of "the violence unleashed into society" by abortion itself and concluded that "violence begets violence."[21]

Another indication of this tendency lies in the hierarchical response to Edward Markley, a Benedictine priest in Alabama who invaded clinics in Birmingham and Huntsville in 1984. Wielding an axe in the Huntsville incident, he injured a clinic employee and was sentenced to prison. His bishop, Joseph Vath, responded by citing Markley as a good priest and pastor. Vath went on to condemn violence but added, "If one is convinced that abortion is the taking of human life according to God's revealed Word, he is not acting unjustly according to God's law in defending the innocent unborn ones." While Markley served his prison term, he was kept as the diocesan head of "pro-life activities."

Representatives of almost every organization in the movement have responded to various bombings and arsons of abortion clinics with statements similar to that of John Burt and David Shofner, a Pensacola coleader, who in response to the 1984 Pensacola bombings as much as said, "I don't approve of violence, but I'm glad it happened" (Blanchard and Prewitt 1993).[22] In sum, while movement organizations may decry the development of sectarian organizations, especially those whose tactics differ from their own, and may highlight the differences in order to maintain or gain membership, when one organization or group in the movement is threatened with sanctions, the others tend to rally to defend it.

The effect of these tendencies is to facilitate interorganizational interactions, support, and even cooperation. A common foe will likely unite disparate groups that would be at one another's throats without an enemy. On the other hand, violence may be counterproductive when third-party support is important because violence tends to alienate third parties (Jenkins 1980:546). With the firm anti-abortionists being a small minority, third-party support is essential to those seeking legal changes, and the violence has clearly not helped them.

Persons who split from an organization to form a new organization have important resources, their ties with persons in the original organization and their knowledge of organizational principles developed through their participation. Their ties with the old organization may also provide a basis for forming linkages and cooperative efforts with the former organization. Personal relationships with the original organization's members may remain sympathetic, providing a basis for those linkages and a degree of mutual support.

As a specific issue arises, a number of divergent groups may be drawn to activity related to it. Thus, it is common for informal, and sometimes formal, coalitions to be formed, usually around a specific problem or issue such as a law before Congress, a case before a court, or persons arrested for demonstrations at a clinic. Such short-term coalitions may be limited to a variety of organizations within a local community, diverse organizations at the national level, or a combination of them, depending on the issue and its newsworthiness.[23] One result of these short-term, issue-specific coalitions is the formation of stronger ties among a wide variety of movement organizations and personnel, facilitating the formation of longer-term, more permanent linkages and coalitions. At the same time, a high degree of competition probably remains among movement organizations for resources such as funds and members.

A number of new organizations have arisen from internal disputes within the movement. Examples are Joseph Scheidler's Pro-Life Action League (established owing to dissatisfaction with the failure of other organizations to be more activist and to his being fired by them), John Willke's Life Issues Institute, and Judie Brown's American Life Institute. Still other organizations have "front groups" to protect them from further legal action, as in the case of Operation Rescue, or to give the illusion of broad-based support for the violent wing, as was the case with the Defenders of the Defenders of Life, a group that amounted to little more than a name on letterhead. Any broadly based social movement such as the anti-abortion movement lends itself to the entrepreneurial development of start-up organizations with specialized interests.

Another factor in this bent toward entrepreneurship lies in the development of new initiatives, tactics, and strategies at different levels of the movement. That is, entrepreneurship appears to encourage greater entrepreneurship in the industry, for each new development in the courts, the legislatures, and movement/countermovement activities opens up new avenues. Small groups with existing common linkages are ready-made for the development of entrepreneurship. While not everyone in such a group will likely move into the new organization or activity, a sufficient core can usually be found to form a cadre for beginning organizational development. This cadre will normally develop a common sense of elitism, a sense of being on the cutting edge, leading where others fear to tread. This common sense of identity is reinforced when the more traditional groups eschew association with the more activist groups. Isolation frees activists from cross-pressures and increases their identification with one another and their tendency toward radicalism (Blanchard and Prewitt 1993).

Yet another factor influencing organizational development is whether the organization is based primarily on a volunteer, part-time, or professional staff. Current research and social movement theory indicate that those organizations with a professional staff have a decided advantage in being able to garner greater resources, wield greater influence in the political arena, and enjoy greater longevity through movement "lows" (Staggenborg 1988 and Fendrich 1984). On the other hand, professional organizations tend to become moderate because of their dependence on outside support, such as that of foundations. They also tend to be less innovative in tactic development, although they facilitate the organization of coalitions (Staggenborg 1988).

Organizational development in the anti-abortion movement demonstrates that the situation may be more complex than theory and previous research reveal. For example, Operation Rescue, while becoming a formal organization, has never really been "professionalized." That is, its leadership is not formally trained. On the other hand, Terry has shown a remarkable ability to avoid negative sanctions and continue organizational activities through a number of creative subterfuges. And he has developed a number of significant coalitions. Similarly, local nonprofessional organizations have been able to establish continuing coalitions among extremely diverse groups, as discussed above. And these local coalitions appear to be connected with a number of national organizations and coalitions, bringing to local events a broad national constituency and resources.

The ability of these groups to bring together such organizational diversity, often with a minimum of professional involvement, and to sustain these interactions and reciprocal supports demands some in-depth research, the goal of which would be to improve our understanding of social movement development under the conditions of organizational professionalization and its absence. Also needed is research on the impact of nonprofessional entrepreneurial organizations and professional ones on each other.

Chapter 7

Modes of Action: The Nature and Impact of Movement Tactics

This chapter looks at the nature of the tactics the anti-abortion movement has employed over its history and at their effectiveness, at the kinds of tactics that tend to be linked with certain individuals and organizations, and at the response these tactics have engendered from the law enforcement community and abortion rights groups.

The Evolution of Movement Tactics and Strategies

As noted in previous chapters, the earliest actions of the anti-abortion movement (prior to 1973) were mild, focusing on the education of church congregations and the general public and on somewhat weak lobbying campaigns to counter the movement for reform and repeal. All of these efforts were conducted under the assumption that most Americans held the view—whether expressed or unexpressed—that abortion was simply wrong. With the success of the campaigns in numerous states to liberalize abortion laws, anti-abortion activists learned that their assumption had been wrong—they could not even count on Catholic legislators to be on their side—and began to seek sources of support. At the same time (the 1970s), the political right wing was looking to unseat what it perceived to be the entrenched liberal power structure, and it sought an alliance with the Christian right. (See, for example, Suall 1962, *The Blue Book of the John Birch Society* 1959, Overstreet 1964, and Landis 1987.) Considerable funds were available from industrialist millionaires such as Adolph Coors for both the religious and political right, and the two forces were ultimately somewhat united in the Moral Majority, as noted in the preceding chapter.

As the mood in the movement became more strident, its tactics became more aggressive; some organizations and/or individuals opted for picketing, blockading, bombing, arson, and, in one instance to date, outright murder. Figure 1 depicts the varied levels of potential involvement of individuals and organizations. Public opinion, what the movement is playing to and relies on, is at the outer edge, with the level of radicalism increasing as one approaches the movement's core. (See note 1 for a more elaborate analysis of figure 1 as it represents the idea of levels of participation in social movements.[1]) Moving from the outer edge to the inner core, the figure also gives a rough approximation of the development of the movement from 1973 to 1988, from groups focusing on education and lobbying to those advocating more radical, sometimes violent, action. There is profound divisiveness within the movement over the proper tactics to use in opposing abortion. The Right to Life Committee has never endorsed Operation Rescue or similar organizations, nor does it report on Operation Rescue activities in its publications. (For an anti-abortionist's qualms about Operation Rescue, see DiSalvo 1989.)

As previously asserted, the first anti-abortion organizations appeared within states in reaction to organization for liberalization of abortion laws. For example, MOMIS, Mothers Outraged at the Murder of Innocents, a Catholic group, was organized in California in 1966 (Lader 1966, 32), and the Association for the Study of Abortion was organized in New York about the same year. These early organizations engaged primarily in educational and lobbying efforts. A few national anti-abortion organizations had been established prior to *Roe v. Wade* and *Doe v. Bolton* in response to the growing national abortion rights movement. These included Americans against Abortion, founded in 1972, Value of Life Committee (1970), Alternatives to Abortion (1971), Birthright (1968), the U.S. Coalition for Life (1972), and Feminists for Life of America (1972).[2] Their efforts differed, some offering alternative options to abortion and support for pregnant women (for example, Alternatives to Abortion), others offering "counseling" about the dangers of abortion (Birthright). Most were engaged in educational and lobbying efforts (Feminists for Life, U.S. Coalition for Life).

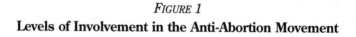

FIGURE 1

Levels of Involvement in the Anti-Abortion Movement

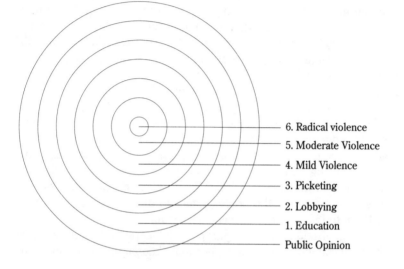

- 6. Radical violence
- 5. Moderate Violence
- 4. Mild Violence
- 3. Picketing
- 2. Lobbying
- 1. Education
- Public Opinion

SOURCE: Blanchard and Prewitt 1993.

With the *Roe v. Wade* and *Doe v. Bolton* decisions in February 1973, the national movement began in earnest. The National Conference of Catholic Bishops had established their Family Life Bureau in 1967 as the pro-choice movement was gathering momentum in various states.[3] After the Supreme Court decisions, that group quickly moved to support and organize the National Right to Life Committee (1973), which, while predominantly Catholic and highly dependent on Catholic funding, is interdenominational. Its initial goal was to have Congress pass a human life amendment to the Constitution. The same goal is espoused by the March for Life (1974), which occurs each year on the anniversary of *Roe v. Wade,* the Life Amendment Political Action Committee (1974), and the National Committee for a Human Life Amendment (1974).

With the failure to get Congress to pass that amendment, efforts began shifting toward electing senators and representatives who would support it. For example, the National Pro-Life Political Action Committee was established in 1977 for that purpose. In addition, as mentioned earlier, the death of the equal rights amendment in 1976 left a large number of anti-ERA organizations and individuals with no cause to support, freeing them to shift their attentions to the abortion issue. While the Moral Majority and other political right organizations took credit for a number of congressional elections and for the defeat of several candidates they opposed, they did not manage the passage of the human life amendment. Various degrees of activism have since arisen.

Perhaps the mildest form of protest is the annual vigil called Life Chain, which arose across the country about 1990. By 1992 some 700 communities were sites for Life Chains (Goodwin 1992). These usually involve several thousand persons gathering in lines along major thoroughfares around a heavy traffic intersection to form a human cross and carrying anti-abortion placards. Such gatherings allow entire families to participate somewhat anonymously in a demonstration. For some persons, this may function as a kind of rite of passage, allowing them to move beyond anti-abortion thoughts, beliefs, and attitudes to a change in behavior, taking an overt, active, and public stance against it. A few of these initiates may then later move toward greater activism and risk taking.[4] For others already engaged in more dramatic demonstrations and picketing, the annual vigil may serve as a rite of intensification and provide a sense of broad support for those other activities.

Again, the general failure of the educational and lobbying efforts mentioned above led to an increase in the activism of the anti-abortion movement beyond relatively passive vigils. In 1980, for example, Joseph Scheidler established his Pro-Life Action League (PLAL), which sponsors picketing and other disruptive activities at clinics. Scheidler's book, *Closed: 99 Ways to Stop Abortion,* while disclaiming support for illegal activities, describes a number of them. It promotes some of the more dramatic picketing tactics, such as the display of full-color pictures of late abortions or stillbirths on posters, buckets of dolls coated with red paint, and thousands of stolen fetuses (Vinzant 1993). He advocates picketing the homes of clinic workers, tracing patients through their license plates and accosting them at home, jamming clinic telephone lines so patients cannot make appointments, and calling people at their homes through the night. In the

1988 presidential campaign he organized disruptions of speeches by Democratic candidate Michael Dukakis and his running mate, Lloyd Bentsen.

Scheidler also maintains contact with those who have been convicted of bombing clinics and has given Protector of Life awards to some of those convicted and sentenced to prison for clinic violence. John Brockhoeft, who traveled to Pensacola, Florida, to bomb the Ladies Center there, met John Burt, the Pensacola activist who showed him the location of the Ladies Center, at a Scheidler event. Several women from San Diego attended a Scheidler training session in Atlanta and returned to organize bombings of San Diego clinics. When I wanted to arrange interviews with those convicted of arsons and bombings across the country, Scheidler's office was able to provide their current addresses. In a conversation with me, an agent of the Bureau of Alcohol, Tobacco, and Firearms who keeps close tabs on anti-abortion organizations confirmed that Scheidler is the central figure in interorganizational cooperation and activities, especially the more "activist" ones.

The failure of picketing and forms of "mild" violence led to an increase of bombings and arsons, which peaked in 1984 and remained relatively high until 1986. The failure of extreme violence to have a significant impact on abortions resulted in the organization of Operation Rescue in 1986. The organization's tactics—which focus on invading and blockading clinics in concerted efforts over a period of weeks or months—lay somewhere between the "mild" violence of stink bombs and glue in locks and the extreme violence of arsons and bombings. Organization cofounder Randall Terry counsels against the use of violence at this time because it is "counterproductive," but he has said, "I believe in violence" (Kurtz 1989).

Other tactics have included selective boycotts. For example, the Christian Action Council announced in August 1990 that it and 24 other anti-abortion groups would boycott American Express and 43 other companies that gave money to Planned Parenthood. American Telephone & Telegraph and 10 other companies consequently announced withdrawal of their support for Planned Parenthood (*Washington Post,* 9 August 1990). Some feminist groups have been able to counteract these efforts. The Minnesota Twin Cities NOW organized a rally and counterboycott of the Dayton Hudson stores (which include Marshall Field) when that company's foundation announced plans to cease donations to Planned Parenthood. The threatened boycott disquieted some stockholders, and the Dayton Foundation reinstated the contribution (Davall 1991).

One of the most effective efforts of the anti-abortion movement was the 1985 film *Silent Scream* (Houston 1985).[5] This film, produced by the Cleveland-based American Life Films, supposedly a sonogram of an actual abortion, was distributed widely, especially among churches. Copies were also sent free to members of Congress and the justices of the Supreme Court. The White House was the setting for Crusade for Life's announcement of the film and its distribution. Ronald Reagan described it as a "chilling documentation of the horrors of abortion" (Houston 1985). While later analyses by pro-choice groups and independent physicians debunked the scientific veracity of the film (see, for example, Prescott 1989 and *Nightline,* 12 February 1985), it made a clear impression on a number of legislators (Cuniberti and Mehren 1985).

The Constituencies behind the Tactics

Factors Linking Individuals with Certain Tactics Those organizations devoted to education and lobbying have tended to be dominated by persons who are upper-middle-class professionals, such as physicians, attorneys, academics, and bishops, cardinals, and ministers. Picketers, however, have tended to be predominantly working-class males and homemakers. Those engaged in bombing and arson have been mainly self-employed working-class males. Operation Rescue activists who have sought arrest have profiles similar to those of the picketers, with occupations that give them time to serve jail sentences and to travel to distant cities.[6] The educational and lobbying organizations appear to be dominated by males, especially in positions of leadership, while women are more active in picketing. Leadership in the picketing and blockading groups tends to be male, however.[7]

A crucial factor in determination of the degree of activism of any individual in the movement appears to be the degree of the person's encapsulation.[8] That is, the more encapsulated the individual, the more likely radical involvement in the movement. Encapsulation refers to the lack of ties to individuals and groups that hold opposing or even disinterested perspectives on the issue of abortion.[9] Those engaged in educational and lobbying activities tend to have professional and other ties with persons and organizations that differ with their abortion stance. Thus, they are caught in cross-pressures that tend to restrain them from radical actions. On the other hand, people such as homemakers and ministers, who are not subject to such occupational pressures, are more open to picketing activities. At the same time, mothers of small children are not likely to risk arrest (Blanchard and Prewitt 1993). Those who have been most violent, the bombers and arsonists, are the least subject to cross-pressures. They tend to be almost totally encapsulated, limiting their relationships to groups who affirm their anti-abortion position and their radical actions. They also tend to be in social positions (single, self-employed, supported by an independent organization) that make a potential prison sentence non-threatening (Blanchard and Prewitt 1993).

The type of organization a person will join and become active in is directly related to his or her social location. The middle class, normally having access to the political system, familiar with "legitimate" political activities, and already active in political organizations, will more frequently choose avenues related to voting and lobbying. As one moves down in social class and also in typical political ties and activities, direct activities become more common. Furthermore, there is an inverse relationship between social class and familiarity with and tolerance of violence. In sum, the nature of an individual's involvement in the movement appears to be a function of sex, occupation, social class, and degree of encapsulation.

Factors Linking Organizations with Certain Tactics   The types of organizations that have developed in the anti-abortion movement may be differentiated in several ways. As mentioned earlier in the text, one distinction may lie in the number of other issues an organization is concerned with. Several, particularly those associated with the Roman Catholic Church, are concerned with the broad range of "pro-life" issues: euthanasia, nuclear weapons, chemical warfare, and the death penalty. Such multi-issue organizations were already in existence at the national level when the 1973 Supreme Court decisions were rendered. Those organizations were therefore in the best position to respond by shifting to mobilize support against abortion specifically. In states where efforts arose to liberalize restrictive abortion laws, single-issue, anti-abortion organizations often arose in response. The networking that had already developed across state lines provided a basis for some of those organizations to go national, in some cases with state organizational representatives coming together to form national structures.

Multi-issue organizations may shift their primary attention from one issue to another, depending on the vagaries of public events. They tend to stress their positions on these events which are in the public eye. Thus, in a real sense, the media set these organizations' agendas. They may shift from the threat of a Three Mile Island or an atomic bomb accidentally dropped from an Air Force plane in Spain to the execution of a John Spinkelink in Florida to the latest abortion statistics. At least partially, this shifting attention arises from the perceived need of an organization to garner increases in membership to improve the public's perception of its power and influence.

Single-issue organizations are often smaller in membership and support, financial and otherwise. At least in the anti-abortion movement, however, it appears that single-issue organizations are more likely to commit themselves to a higher level of activism than are multi-issue ones. Indeed, the smaller the organization, the greater risk members appear willing to take. Of course, by their nature, high-risk organizations are less likely to be able to garner broad membership and support.[10]

Another type of movement organization is what Gamson (1992:62–63) calls the "affinity group," a small group that "takes responsibility for activating its own members and participates as a unit in collective action." The Lambs for Christ, local Operation Rescue units, Rescue America, and Missionaries to the Unborn fit this type.

The Functions and Effects of Violence

As indicated by Killian (1972:41), the more violent wing of a social movement may have several divergent effects on and uses to it. Killian points out that "extremism" in a social movement may have several possible outcomes. It may "(1) increase the bargaining power of moderate leaders; (2) provide a corrective to illusions of progress by (3) identifying unresolved issues and defining new ones; (4) radicalize a growing segment of the movement membership and increase the polarization between the movement and its opposition; (5) focus the attention of the opposition and the bystander public on new issues; and (6) evoke extreme repressive measures from the opposition." All these effects may be found in various organizations within the anti-abortion movement at different times and stages of its development. We will now examine Killian's propositions with specific reference to the movement.

The increase of bargaining power among the more moderate leaders resulting from the clinic bombings and arsons is demonstrated by Ronald Reagan's reception at the White House in 1985, following the annual February March for Life, of a large number of anti-abortion leaders, including Joseph Scheidler. At that meeting, as mentioned in chapter 6, Scheidler requested pardons for several bombers, and Reagan reportedly said he would consider them on a case-by-case basis.

There had been an illusion of progress toward the movement's goals. The Moral Majority was formed in 1979, giving a new sense of unity and power to many in the movement. In 1980, in *Harris v. McRae,* the Supreme Court upheld the Hyde Amendment, forbidding the use of federal funds for abortions. In 1982 Reagan publicly endorsed the prayer amendment (which would nullify Supreme Court decisions forbidding prayer in public schools) and tax credits for private schools, and he "wrote a conciliatory letter to anti-abortion movement leaders" (Diamond 1989:64). In 1983, in *Kansas City v. Ashcroft,* the Supreme Court approved the parental consent requirement for minors as long as an alternative method of approval was available to them. In May 1984, the Hyde Amendment was extended to ban federal funds for international family planning agencies promoting or funding abortion. Yet all these events failed to perceptibly slow the rate of abortions being performed in the United States.

The increase in clinic arsons and bombings in 1983–84, as well as other less violent activities, clearly were a response to a lack of progress in curbing abortions at the end of Reagan's first term (Blanchard and Prewitt 1993). As mentioned in chapter 5, they appear to be a frustrated response to the rising expectations initiated by the Reagan election and the original hopes for the pro-life amendment.[11] The frustration resulting from a perceived lack of real progress in reducing abortions led to more dramatic actions.

Polarization and radicalization resulted from the violence, with both an increasing support for the pro-choice movement and a decline in those participating in demonstrations and picketing in 1985–87 (Blanchard and Prewitt 1993). One illustration of this occurred in New Orleans during the picketing of the 1985 national meeting of the National Organization for Women, when local organizers asked John Burt, who had brought with him a five-month-old fetus named Baby Charlie, to get out of the picket line. The New Orleans leaders did not want to be identified with behavior that could be seen by the public as offensive. That is, those who engaged primarily in picketing tended to either (1) reinforce their commitment to that type of activity or (2) withdraw from those activities to distance themselves from those who appeared to the public to be more radical. Thus, while the number of picketers appeared to decline as more radical actions grew, those who continued picketing appeared to renew and deepen their commitment to that type of activity. At the same time, general public support for abortion rights underwent a slight but statistically significant decline between 1980 and 1985 (Gillespie 1988).

New issues raised by the violence included, at the least, the depth of commitment of some segments of the movement. As a result of the media coverage of the radical actions, the public began to increasingly perceive the abortion issue as a more volatile one. Many in the general public apparently began re-examining their own positions and drawing finer distinctions among the conditions under which they considered abortion to be an acceptable choice. The violence also led to criticism in numerous newspaper editorials. Many in the public questioned how "pro-life" could also mean destroying property and thereby possibly harming people.

Repressive measures may arise, as Killian asserts, from the countermovement, but they may also arise from official sources, as was the case with the repression of the early union movement in the late 1800s and early 1900s by the federal government. Repression evoked by the violence included the initial condemnation of the violence by Reagan in January 1985 and the number of unprecedented trials and convictions of clinic bombers and arsonists in that year. A quieting of "extreme" activism also followed a federal judge's injunctions and jailings of Operation Rescue protesters in Wichita, Kansas, in 1991. Joseph Scheidler also retired to background activities after the National Organization for Women and two clinics filed suit against him and others under RICO (Racketeer Influenced Corrupt Organizations) laws. As federal courts at higher and higher levels upheld judgments against the movement, Scheidler appeared to retreat.

While Randall Terry and Operation Rescue arose in the late 1980s to replace Scheidler's leadership, they were soon brought into the same court suits. Adverse judgments, especially in New York, led Terry to use subterfuges to avoid their effects. He kept funds in a personal account to avoid the courts. Later, other organizations were established to handle the Operation Rescue funds. In 1992, for example, he established the American Anti-Persecution League to "sue anyone who violates a prolife demonstrator's civil rights" (Planned Parenthood 1992d).

The Backlash against Movement Tactics

Local law enforcement responses to anti-abortion activities have varied widely. In some communities, one or more judges have been overtly against abortion, giving ordinance violators minimum fines or sentences, if any at all. Some judges have even accepted the necessity defense, the proposition that blockades are a legitimate activity in preventing the death of a fetus.

Where activities such as those of Operation Rescue have been prolonged and vituperative, there has been a tendency for local law enforcement officials to grow weary and to escalate the punishments meted out. By 1990 activists were protesting the longer jail terms being exacted. They were particularly angry over the pain-compliance techniques used in the arrests of noncooperative demonstrators. Pain-compliance (inflicting pain to compel compliance with arrest) appears to be most readily used by larger urban police forces, such as Los Angeles, West Hartford, and Atlanta.

In 1980 Abortion Rights Mobilization and about 20 abortion rights groups filed a federal court suit against the Internal Revenue Service to revoke the federal tax exemption of the U.S. Catholic Conference and the National Conference of Catholic Bishops on the grounds that both groups used their funds to affect legislation. While the two church organizations were included in the original suit as defendants, they were removed by the Manhattan District Court in 1989. This left only the IRS as a defendant for the alleged failure to revoke the tax exemption of the religious organizations. The case wound its way through the various levels of federal courts, including plaintiff charges of contempt of court because the Catholic groups would not release internal financial documents, until it was resolved in 1992 by the Supreme Court, which upheld the tax-exempt status of the church organizations. Nonetheless, lower-court decisions against the Bishops' Conference and the appeal processes had absorbed their attention and financial resources for 12 years.

In 1987, Michael and Linda Franson, residents of Oregon, had a girl born with severe cerebral defects and unable to take food. Physicians "recommended that extraordinary measures not be taken to keep the baby alive" (*New York Times,* 12 December 1987), and the parents concurred. Right to Life Oregon (RTLO) then got a court order requiring the hospital to provide life support for the infant, who died anyway in a week. The Fransons sued RTLO for interference with their "parental custody" after the Portland hospital billed them for about $10,000 for the week's maintenance of the baby. RTLO's insurer insisted on settling the case for $217,500.

Political activities against the anti-abortion movement have included the support of pro-choice politicians, especially those facing anti-abortion incumbents, and major efforts to defeat state referenda attempting to limit abortion access, especially in Massachusetts, Rhode Island, Arkansas, and Oregon in 1986. The same election season saw the election of several pro-choice candidates to the House and the Senate (Greenhouse 1986).

One pro-choice reaction to the political and demonstrative efforts of the anti-abortion movement, including the distribution of the film *Silent Scream,* was its "Silent No More" campaign. This involved women and men "coming out" and publicly stating the positive effects of abortion on their lives, as well as the negative effects of illegal abortions. The campaign involved a number of celebrities to add legitimacy to abortion (Brozan 1985 and Cuniberti and Mehren 1985). The willingness of individuals to admit that they had sought illegal abortions prior to *Roe* and *Doe* had an impact on the media and, presumably, on the public.

Another tactic of the pro-choicers that began to bear fruit in threatening anti-abortion protesters at clinics in the late 1980s and early 1990s was the use of federal court injunctions against disorderly demonstrations. A federal appeals court in 1988 upheld an injunction against a demonstrating organization in Portland, Oregon. Even more dramatic was the judgment of contempt by a federal judge in Wichita, Kansas, in 1992, mentioned earlier in the text. The judge not only levied heavy fines against persons and organizations in the demonstrations there, sponsored primarily by Operation Rescue, but determined that the fines would be turned over to the clinics that had been the object of the demonstrations. Subsequent demonstrations in Buffalo, New York, in 1992 were scheduled for a full month, but fell apart after only eight days.

The most successful strategy of the abortion rights movement to date has been its suits against picketing and invading organizations and individual organizers of the anti-abortion movement under federal RICO and the so-called Ku Klux Klan Act (which forbade acts against classes of persons, such as African-Americans; suits brought by the abortion rights movement under this act seek to define attempts to close clinics as acts against women as a class). The first such suit was filed by the Pensacola, Florida, Ladies Center Clinic, the National Organization for Women, and a Wilmington, Delaware, clinic in 1986 with the assistance of the Southern Poverty Law Center of Montgomery, Alabama, which later withdrew from the suit. Defendants included Joseph Scheidler and his National Pro-Life Action League (Herbers 1986).[12] As mentioned above, the suit appeared to force Scheidler to move into the background of protests. In March 1989 Randall Terry and Operation Rescue were added to the suit. Eventually, more than 10 such RICO and anti-Ku Klux Klan suits were filed against various protestors and protesting organizations. In 1989 the Third District Court of Appeals upheld a Philadelphia jury verdict that anti-abortion protesters had "embarked on a willful campaign to use fear, harassment, intimidation and force against [a] clinic" (Ireland 1989). Civil rights laws were also used in *Alexandria Women's Health Clinic v. Bray,* with charges that Bray and others conspired to deprive women of a constitutional right, access to abortion. The primary defendants in this case are also related to Operation Rescue. That case is also still under appeal by the defendants to higher courts.[13] Suits against Operation Rescue in New York alone resulted in fines amounting to more than $450,000 in 1990 (Suh and Denworth 1989). The Florida office was forced to close because of the heavy fines against it. The national office closed in 1990 because of $475,000 in fines. The NOW case was heard by the Supreme Court in 1991, and NOW won injunctions and fines in Oregon, California, Massachusetts, Pennsylvania, New York, and Florida. In 1992, the Supreme Court ruled that RICO and KKK laws do not apply in cases like those brought by abortion rights activists.

Additional legal recourse for clinics and physicians may lie in the anti-stalking laws many states began to enact in the early 1990s. These laws are intended to protect persons from "stalkers," usually men who obsessively follow and monitor women, sometimes with the goal of physically harming or killing them. The ineffectiveness of injunctions and the fact that most current laws require some overt act before a dangerous person can be arrested have made the need for such laws apparent. Judie Brown of the American Life League announced in 1992 a campaign against such laws because they "could be used to thwart pro-life non-violent direct action" (Planned Parenthood 1992j). Presumably, anti-stalking laws could be used to prosecute those who follow and harass abortion providers or who locate the home and work locations of women seeking abortions and contact their neighbors or relatives. States' enactment of 24-hour waiting periods for women between requesting and having an abortion have increased the likelihood of such "stalking."

These court suits and trials, of course, cost the anti-abortion movement organizations and individuals involved a great deal of money in defending themselves and appealing their cases. They also caused Operation Rescue, in effect, to go "underground." As mentioned earlier, Operation Rescue virtually disappeared as a formal organization and Randall Terry ran all its funds through his personal bank account to keep them from being seized by the courts; this in turn made those contributions taxable. On the other hand, it appears that these court defeats also led to a multiplication of other, substitute, ad hoc organizations to fill the vacuum, such as the Lambs for Christ and Missionaries to the Pre-Born, as well the decentralization of Operation Rescue into local and state organizations. Other organizations, some already established and others apparently established for that purpose, arose to solicit funds for Operation Rescue. For example, the Committee to Protect the Family Foundation solicited funds in 1990 to pay off Operation Rescue's $40,000 debts in operating and payroll expenses (Pratt 1990).

Further backlash against Operation Rescue and those using similar tactics arose in cities and counties that had been the focus of their demonstrations to enact stronger laws and punishments for such activities. For example, the Cincinnati city council moved in May 1992 to enact mandatory jail sentences of 3 to 12 days, depending on the number of convictions, for those "trespassing on the grounds of medical facilities" (Planned Parenthood 1992f). An Iowa and a Wisconsin community enacted legislation forbidding picketing of specific residences (Planned Parenthood 1992f). Laws against clinic blockades were enacted in Denver and San Jose, California (Planned Parenthood 1992h). The city of Baton Rouge erected a six-foot fence around a targeted clinic there. The fence thwarted Operation Rescue efforts to blockade the clinic (Planned Parenthood 1992i). Similarly, a snow fence was erected in Wichita (Planned Parenthood 1992g).

The Strategic Use of Rhetoric and Symbolic Action

For our purposes it is sufficient to indicate the major efforts to utilize rhetoric as a recruiting and political device.[14] In effect, both sides of the abortion debate attempt to use rhetoric to appeal to key values of the American populace and thereby influence political events as well as individual behaviors. That is, rhetoric is a form of propaganda, which is designed not so much to change persons' thinking as their behavior (Ellul 1965). The rhetoric of both the pro-choice and anti-abortion movements seeks to build a (1) supportive public opinion, which will in turn (2) influence political actions and laws, and to (3) influence women in their abortion decisions. As Gamson (1992:70–71) has pointed out, this process requires "framing" (Goffman 1974) the issue in terms that "resonate with cultural narrations; that is, with the stories, myths, and folk tales that are part and parcel of one's cultural heritage and thus function to inform events and experiences in the immediate present" (Snow and Benford 1988:210).

Rhetoric serves the additional goal of maintaining and heightening the commitment of already converted adherents. Rhetoric, then, functions as a rite of both maintenance and intensification. A good example of this lies in the responses of both the anti-abortion and pro-choice organizational representatives to the *Planned Parenthood of Southeastern Pennsylvania v. Casey* 1992 Supreme Court decision. NOW used the decision to try to encourage membership renewals and broaden its membership by characterizing the decision as the death of *Roe.* Randall Terry and other anti-abortion leaders used the decision to the same ends for their organizations by bemoaning the court's explicit statement that *Roe* still stands. Both sides tend to decry any Supreme Court decision as a major defeat, thereby characterizing their goals as in danger in order to motivate support and raise funds.

Rhetoric involves, of course, the careful selection of terminology to cast one's own side in the most favorable light and the opposition in the most unfavorable. It is a use of symbolic power, a powerful and yet relatively nonalienating form of power (Etzioni 1968), a manipulation of values. For example, the anti-abortion movement's seizure of terms such as *pro-life* and *pro-family* implies that the opposition is *pro-death* and *anti-family.*

A number of rhetorical terms has been stressed by the anti-abortion movement. Members commonly refer to abortion as another *Holocaust,* abortion providers as *pro-abortionists, baby killers, covens of witches,* and *murderers* (Lake 1986, Van Winden 1988, Diamond 1989, Blanchard and Prewitt 1993). Appeal to the imagery of the Holocaust led to the characterization of abortion as *genocide;* this idea was seized on particularly by African-Americans in the movement, charging that the genocide was directed primarily at their future children. Abortion is *legalized murder.* Women seeking abortions are urged, do not *murder your baby.* Anti-abortionists often refer to clinics as *abortuaries* and *death camps* (Blanchard and Prewitt 1993). While physicians speak of *zygotes* and *fetuses,* anti-abortionists refer to *babies* and *pre-borns* (Tumulty 1989). Ronald Reagan and some in the movement refer to the *unborn.* Robert Packwood, Republican senator from Oregon, has been termed *Senator Death* for his support of choice.

M_anwhile, the pro-choice movement refers to *tissue, products of conception,* and *choice;* abortionists are *providers;* and Operation Rescue is *Operation Oppress-You.* In the mid-1970s in Dallas, Texas, choice advocates consciously chose the term *fetus* and rejected the use of *child* to counteract anti-abortion rhetoric. Later, pro-choicers became careful to use a variety of terms: *embryo* during the eight-week period of gestation; *fetus* from the ninth week to birth. They rejected the previously used *pro-abortion* in favor of *pro-choice.* One of their early pamphlets, "Abortion by Choice," was later changed to "Motherhood by Choice" (Faux 1988:126). Jimmye Kimmey coined the usage *pro-choice* while coordinating briefs for *Roe v. Wade,* and *abortion on request* as opposed to *abortion on demand* (Faux 1988:235).

Clearly, the two groups are appealing to conflicting sets of values, the anti-abortionists to the notion of traditional "family," large families, and an implicit control of women. On the other hand, the pro-choice movement is appealing to more contemporary values of sexual equality, self-realization, self-actualization, female achievement, and individual freedom ("choice"), among others. The ambivalence of the "mushy middle" of the American public on the conditions under which abortion is acceptable reflects their indecision before historical but conflicting basic values.

The rhetoric of the anti-abortion movement sometimes goes beyond the appeal to basic values. For example, some members of the movement, particularly Protestant fundamentalists, ascribe abortion to a conspiracy of secular humanists (Vanderford 1989, Koop and Schaeffer 1983, LaHaye 1983). Others have blamed it on historical American Protestantism's anti-Catholicism (Nathanson 1983). The National Right to Life Committee used the conspiracy appeal, for example, to gain new members by charging that the three major television networks, ABC, NBC, and CBS, have conspired to ignore the realities of abortion in the United States and to support abortion (Franz 1992).

Uses of the media by the anti-abortion movement go beyond selective choice of terminology to garner support; they also include variations in the style of presenting arguments. At one extreme, there is the 1992 DeMoss Foundation soft-sell television ads depicting active and happy children, pregnant women, cheerful families, and even one teenage girl claiming to be a failed late-term abortion—all with the theme "choose life." At the other extreme, during the 1992 political campaigns, several candidates for various state legislatures showed explicit pictures of aborted fetuses in their campaign ads. Federal election laws made it illegal for television stations to refuse to carry the ads (Mimi Hall 1992).[15] It is possible and even likely that in future political campaigns some segments of the anti-abortion movement may field candidates not necessarily to get them elected but to take advantage of the election laws to sponsor television advertising that might be otherwise rejected.[16]

A step beyond the use of rhetoric is the use of symbolic actions, which have the same basic motivations as rhetoric, with the additional goal of reducing abortion options. Baby Charlie, the fetus displayed by John Burt in a 1985 picket line in New Orleans, is an example of a symbol; in displaying it Burt wanted to shock ambivalent people and to convince them of the humanity of the fetus. Like rhetoric, symbols are a form of propaganda. Similar symbolic actions include the relatively quiet picketing and praying in front of clinics, offices, and courthouses and the annual March for Life in Washington, D.C.

These types of symbolic action have the effect of moderately alienating the opposition, but they also have minor negative effects on the wavering public. The picketing at clinics and offices probably acts as a slight deterrent to women coming to them for abortions or other services. On the other hand, it requires such prolonged commitment and effort on the part of the participants that it may soon loose its allure and the number of picketers will decline, information that will have a negative effect on the movement's public image. Thus, there is a tendency for the level of symbolic action to increase in order to renew commitment of the activists and secure new recruits.[17] Escalation can also result from the frustration of unrealized expectations (Blanchard and Prewitt 1993).

The next level of symbolic actions, such as picketing physicians' homes, demonstrating against them in airports as they depart and arrive, and picketing patients' homes, affect the availability of abortion. These actions inhibit women from seeking abortions for fear of exposure, and they inhibit physicians from performing abortions.[18] It is particularly inhibitive on the availability of abortion services in rural communities. Abortion services are available in only 17 percent of the nation's counties and virtually all are in urban centers.

The movement to "mildly" illegal activities is a short step for some persons. Stink bombs, glue in locks, threatening telephone calls to clinics and their personnel, and clinic blockades are examples of this form of intimidation. An employee of a Washington, D.C., hospital disclosed names and telephone numbers of women scheduled for abortions to an area anti-abortion leader, Olga Fairfax, who then went to their homes to try to dissuade them from having the abortion by showing them slides and a jar with 12 fetuses in it (Weiser 1985). A man next door to a Kansas City clinic who asked demonstrators to lower the volume of their bullhorn was beaten with fists and signs (Planned Parenthood 1992f).

Such acts further inhibit the availability of abortion, since it is difficult for most people to continue for long under such threats. The convictions of those who break the law also have symbolic implications. Being fined or sentenced to jail not only has symbolic significance to the outside world of a degree of commitment to a cause, it also tends to increase the commitment of the person sanctioned, for the more one sacrifices to a cause, the greater the commitment tends to become (Kanter 1972). The research of Blanchard and Prewitt (1993), for example, indicates that the majority of those who have been sentenced to prison for bombing or setting fire to clinics have remained active in the movement, although usually being careful not to commit additional illegal acts.

Movement Organization Responses to Violence and Radical Actions

Officially, the moderate, professional anti-abortion organizations condemn violence, as already indicated. But virtually everyone of them does this in an equivocal manner. That is, while they condemn the violence, they also publicly give thanks for it. For example, support for violence came at the 1981 National Right to Life Committee meeting at Disney World, people "bowed their heads at one point and prayed the Lord would 'send the enemy to the pit of destruction'" and "enthusiastically applauded indirect references to vandalism and arson at abortion clinics" (English 1981:16).[19]

Richard Doerflinger, assistant director of the Office of Prolife Activities of the National Conference of Catholic Bishops, said that "protests that have sometimes culminated in violence, and are galvanizing new action among groups that support women's right to choose abortions, do not reflect mainstream antiabortion strategy" (Brozan 1985). On the other hand, as we have already noted, the National Bishops Conference has blamed clinic bombings on the existence of abortion clinics. The head of the National Right to Life Committee, Dr. John C. Willke, asked, "Who are these folks? Not wild-eyed bombers. They come right out of the local Christian church. They do it as a present for Christ." Joseph Scheidler calls the bombers "good Christians."

The response of some anti-abortion organizations and individual activists to the murder of Dr. David Gunn and the wounding of Dr. George Tiller in 1993 is also noteworthy. On 10 March 1993 Michael Griffin of Pensacola, Florida, admittedly shot Dr. David Gunn in the back three times and killed him as Gunn was entering a Pensacola clinic to begin work for the day. Griffin had picketed the clinic during the prior month with John Burt's local group, a branch of Rescue America. Griffin had also viewed anti-abortion videotapes, among them *The Hard Truth*, at John Burt's Our Father's House and had attended a nearby fundamentalist church with Burt the Sunday before the shooting.

In August 1993 Rachelle Shannon of Oregon shot Dr. George Tiller as he was about to drive away from his clinic in Wichita, Kansas. Tiller was wounded slightly in both arms and able to resume his practice the next day. Shannon had corresponded frequently with Griffin after Griffin's arrest, and Griffin had called her collect from jail at least once. In her letters to him, she praised Griffin and called him a hero. She had also edited "The Brockhoeft Report," a newsletter devoted to convicted clinic bomber John Brockhoeft, who, as mentioned in chapter 6, was sentenced to prison for on bombing-related charges.

Anti-abortion organizations quickly moved to distance themselves from the acts of Griffin and Tiller. For the first time, the National Right to Life Committee and similar organizations were unequivocal in their denunciations. But there quickly arose several persons and groups to defend the murder of physicians performing abortions. The murders were an escalation of violence, and the defense of them was a matching escalation of the rhetoric.

David Trosch, a Catholic priest and pastor of the Magnolia Springs, Alabama, parish, located about 35 miles from Pensacola, attempted to place an advertisement with a crude drawing of someone shooting an abortionist in the Mobile and Pensacola newspapers. The drawing was labeled, "Justifiable Homicide," and both papers rejected it. The papers did, however, run stories on the event and interviews with Trosch. Trosch's bishop, Oscar Lipscomb of the Mobile diocese, ordered Trosch to remain silent on the issue because his stance violated the canons of the church. Subsequent to Trosch's granting another press interview, Lipscomb relieved Trosch of his pastoral duties and reassigned him to a period of "contemplation."

A number of others added their voices to Trosch's. Paul Hill, an excommunicated minister of an independent Presbyterian church, who had moved to Pensacola and joined Burt's picketers, appeared on *The Phil Donahue Show* defending the killing of abortionists (Hill 1993). He also organized a group called Defensive Action, which he described as a small group of men across the country, to advocate more murders.

The Portland, Oregon, Life Advocates issued several statements supporting such actions (deParrie 1993, McCullough 1993). One of those writing for Life Advocates was Gary McCullough, a national leader of Operation Rescue (McCullough 1993). The *Capitol Area Christian News* had in December 1992 already published an article detailing the uses of butyric acid on clinics and describing its effects. The same issue supported bombings and arsons, while condemning those anti-abortionists disavowing violence.

Clearly, the more moderate organization leaders find benefits in at least some kinds of violence but feel a necessity to distance themselves from it. It appears they are seeking to claim the benefits of radical action while disavowing responsibility for it.

Chapter 8

An Interactive Dynamic: Technological and Social Change vis à vis the Anti-Abortion Movement

The numerous technological and social changes characterizing the twentieth century have, not surprisingly, had an impact on the character of the anti-abortion movement. This chapter considers the issues raised for consideration by the movement as a result of technical developments in medicine, communications, and computer networks and of such social phenomena as urbanization.

Medical Technology

For the anti-abortion movement, troublesome developments in medical technology are those related to conception and birth, life sustenance and death. The most troublesome issue, of course, is the development of relatively safe methods of abortion, methods that can be easily and effectively administered by even nonphysicians with little training. Most factions of the movement have opposed the new technologies related to fertility control, both methods of contraception and of assisting in conception. It appears that a "natural theology" underlies the major elements of the movement, both Catholic and fundamentalist Protestant,[1] and this leads many of its adherents to oppose any method of fertility control or assistance that deviates from "natural" sexual congress and the chances of conception associated with it. These stances reveal almost more than anything else the religious ideology that underlies and motivates the core of the movement's activist wing.

Of course, the development of the sonogram gave the movement a powerful propaganda tool, which it put to effective use in *Silent Scream.* Thus, while the movement generally abhors modernism and secularization, as well as the technological developments that have gone hand-in-glove with them, it does not hesitate to use products of these advances for its own cause

Communications Media

Among the products of technological change most useful to the anti-abortion movement have been modern communications media. Evangelists discovered radio early in its history. They used it to raise funds and to create a regional or national audience of adherents.[2] Evangelists found that radio exposure created larger audiences for them in local revivals. Thus, radio programs and personal appearances were mutually reinforcing. One aspect of secularization is that it increases competition among religious groups. As D. L. Munby (1963) indicated, a secular society has no official meaning system; the individual is expected to find his or her own. This places religion and values in the marketplace as things that have to be "sold." Evangelicals and fundamentalists have become masters of advertising.

The development of television proved particularly beneficial. While most fundamentalists eschewed television as a tool of the devil and equated it with movies during the 1950s, when television first began spreading across the nation, they soon learned how to use it. An early entrepreneur in the use of television was Billy James Hargis, an Arkansas-based evangelist and the head of the Christian Crusade, a right-wing anti-communist organization that rode on the coattails of McCarthyism. Hargis later tried to pick up on the anti-abortion movement, but was not successful in his efforts. Billy Graham was also a leader in using television to get a larger audience for his crusades. Other evangelists saw an opportunity for regular and weekly exposure for broadened financial support. Soon ministers such as Oral Roberts began appearing regularly on television. Their soaring income inspired others to seek this wider ministry.

The introduction and widespread expansion of cable television in the 1980s and 1990s brought new opportunities. Pat Robertson established the Christian Broadcasting Network (CBN), and others evangelical groups established local Christian stations that have found cable essential to their building an audience, since most could not afford strong signal stations. These stations are avenues for various evangelical and fundamentalist programs. In the 1990s hardly an hour of daytime programming is available on these stations.[3]

Evangelical/fundamentalist presentations have changed through time. Oral Roberts, for example, concentrated on healing in his early programs. As it became evident that the more "radical" religious expressions turned off a large number of people, evangelists learned to temper their religious expressions to appeal to a broader audience. The more controversial expressions were relegated to untelevised appearances and services. In sum, they learned how to market their product to a wider audience.[4]

Evangelists also began to use more sophisticated advertising techniques, assisted by upscale advertising agencies (Cuniberti and Mehren 1985). While decrying the display of sexuality in network and secular television, they began using it themselves, although in a subtle way. It is virtually impossible to find an evangelical program that does not zoom in on attractive, young women in the choir or congregation, much as the cameras do at football games. Evangelists also increasingly use the appearances of their wives to add sex appeal to their programs. Tammy Bakker is one of the more obvious examples.

Furthermore, while decrying the violence of the network shows, Robertson's Christian Broadcasting Network has on its regular weekend schedule of "family" television reruns of *The Rifleman, Wagon Train, Laramie, Cimarron Strip, Branded, Laredo, I Spy, The Cisco Kid,* and *The Lone Ranger*—mostly westerns centered on violent encounters between "pure" good and evil, white hats versus black hats. Indeed, the National Coalition on Television Violence (NCTV), which regularly monitors television broadcasting and grades programs, recently made this comment about the Christian Broadcasting Network:

NCTV has expressed its concern to CBN drama-action programming. Despite our best efforts, CBN has not been willing to meet with us to study this issue. NCTV has congratulated CBN on the low level of violence on its Monday through Friday daytime entertainment. However, Saturdays from 9 A.M. to 9 P.M. and Sunday 1 P.M. to 6 P.M. violent western programming takes over.

Also, *The Rifleman* and *Man from U.N.C.L.E.* appear five days a week in early and late-evening programming.

It is about this programming that NCTV has the most concern. During these hours on Saturday and Sunday, CBN has the highest number of acts of violence per hour of any network in America. Although the violence is not as gruesome or vicious as in some pay-cable movies, it is an issue of concern (*Pensacola News Journal,* 25 October 1986, 7C).

NCTV reports that CBN defends this programming as "helping fund the CBN ministry and thus bringing more people to Christ." This utilitarian ethic, soundly rejected by mainstream Christian denominations and, in theory, by most fundamentalists as well as most secular humanists, justifies the means used by the ends sought. It is the same justification given by those performing violence against the clinics and physicians' offices.

These stations and networks have become important sources for promoting the anti-abortion movement. Some organizations, such as the American Life League, have even established regular programs for promoting their activities and goals to a national audience, building a larger constituency while seeking broader funding sources. The movement has also used the three major national networks, ABC, CBS, and NBC, especially their news divisions, extensively. Organizations have learned to use the dramatic event and the sound bite, the pithy, quotable statement, to draw media attention. The confrontations of clinic blockaders and police, the display of an aborted fetus preserved in formaldehyde, a group kneeling and praying with raised hands on courthouse steps, a clinic blazing or flattened by a bomb—all are at least partially designed to grab a moment or two on local or national television or an article in the newspaper.

The media—newspapers, radio, and especially television—have given the movement tools for spreading its message, soliciting recruits and funds, dramatizing its message, and antagonizing and sometimes frustrating the opposition. At least one effect of media attention to the staging of events is to recruit new members nationwide, drawing these persons away from other, indigenous local movement organizations (Maxwell 1992). By installing 800 telephone numbers and encouraging viewers to call in for prayer, to call to make pledges, televangelists have also expanded their mailing lists, enabling them to hit people twice, once on television and then many times through the mails.

There is also at least one organization, American Life Films, that devotes itself to the production of anti-abortion videos, which are widely promoted and viewed, especially among anti-abortion churches. One of these videos, *Assignment Life,* a simulated reporter's investigation into the "reality" of abortion, was blamed by the defense in the trial of the Pensacola Four as one of the major influences that led them to bomb three clinics in Pensacola on Christmas morning in 1984 (Blanchard and Prewitt 1993). As noted in chapter 7, this organization also produced *Silent Scream.* (See *48 Hours,* 11 August 1993.)

Print media have also been an important tool of the movement. Brochures, tracts, and such have grown increasingly sophisticated. There has been wide distribution of a number of items depicting fetuses in living color, sometimes improperly disposed of in dumpsters and vacant lots. These are often juxtaposed in the same publication with quotations from authorities, such as portions of Ronald Reagan's essay against abortion, a favorite passage from it being, "Something must be done." These publications have a tabloid feel to them and seem designed to appeal to a similar audience. In addition, virtually every anti-abortion organization has its own periodical publication to publicize events. They also report on the activities of other organizations, even those whose tactics they oppose, thereby giving tacit support to them (Neitz 1981).

Perhaps the most dramatic development in the movement's use of the media was the Catholic Bishops' Conference hiring of the Hill and Knowlton public relations firm to manage its $5 million anti-abortion campaign (Steinfels 1990), as mentioned in chapter 6. There was a loud outcry against this tactic and its funding by the Knights of Columbus. In January 1992, the Bishops' Conference canceled its contract with Hill and Knowlton and began negotiations with a new firm composed of "disgruntled Hill and Knowlton employees" (Planned Parenthood 1992c).

Urbanization

Urbanization, a primary mark of economic and social development, has been a basic asset of the movement. The vast majority of abortions occur in urban centers. Urbanization is accompanied by an anonymity unimaginable in rural communities. In Pensacola, Florida, for example, about 75 percent of obstetricians/gynecologists perform abortions for their regular patients in their offices, but if a nonclient calls the office and asks if abortions are performed there, the response is no. Doctors can thus perform abortions with limited awareness on the part of the general public. At the same time, clients in an urban environment are not likely to bump into an acquaintance who will tell others of the encounter. In medium-size communities those seeking abortions frequently travel to a neighboring community, where they feel their privacy is more or less assured. Clinics, as mentioned previously, will frequently import physicians to perform their abortions, since local physicians are more subject to sanctions. Some anti-abortion movement organizations have developed techniques for following these physicians to their home communities and publicizing there their out-of-town activities.

A primary factor in making urbanization a factor in abortion lies in its legalization. Prior to *Roe* and *Doe,* it appears that a number of small-town, as well as urban, physicians performed abortions virtually on demand. This practice was probably due at least partially to rural physicians' close relationships with and dependence on the families in their community. For example, I discovered that a hospital in Crestview, Florida, and a physician in Century, Florida, were performing abortions in the 1940s (Blanchard and Prewitt 1993). This was generally known in those and surrounding communities. Fundamentalists did not, to my knowledge, picket them or inform the authorities about them.[5] Their primary concern is not the *occurrence* of abortion but its *legalization,* which gives it the stamp of legal and, more important, moral approval.[6] Thus, legalization has probably led to a decline in the rural availability of abortion and made it a largely urban phenomenon. In a sense, then, while legalization has made abortion much more affordable, it has also probably localized its availability to urban areas, and this is due primarily to stigmatization by the anti-abortion movement.

Legalization also allowed for the development of clinics. *Roe* decreed that abortions in the first trimester could occur outside hospitals. The majority of clinics are located in individual buildings, rather than high-rise medical facilities, and on main thoroughfares. They also advertise in the Yellow Pages and newspaper want-ads. That is, they are easy to locate and isolate, ready targets for picketing, bombings, arsons, and other forms of harassment. They are ready-made, easy targets for the movement.

Technology and Outreach

As indicated earlier, a primary factor in the increasing visibility and media coverage of the movement was the establishment of the Moral Majority. The computerized mailing lists generated by Richard Vigurie for the Moral Majority enabled it to target an enormous number of organizations and individuals to secure funding. Mailing lists have been traded, sold, and swapped among right-wing organizations with varied agendas, enabling them to build their constituencies. Refined programs enable organizations to merge the data on those who respond to their mailings to create ever more precise and targeted lists for future mailings. Membership lists become economic assets for sale to other organizations and commercial entrepreneurs.

Computers also allow organizations to inflate estimates of their constituencies. For example, one may write, as I have, to an organization for information and be placed on its regular mailing list and probably be counted as a supporter or even a member. Once on a mailing list, one has to go to extra effort to get off it, because numbers count in getting dollars from large contributors, particularly foundations.

Technology and Social Control

Technology has also played a role in efforts to control the more radical elements of the movement. For example, the FBI maintains computerized files on key activists, as do local police departments on those in their communities. Also, elements of the pro-choice movement maintain records on national activists such as Randall Terry and Joseph Scheidler. Indeed, one such source sent to an Atlanta judge the record of Terry's arrests across the country, which reportedly became a primary basis for the judge's decision to keep Terry in jail as long as he did.

Networks of computerized data have allowed various local and federal policing agencies to identify law breakers in the movement and bring them to trial. Various policing jurisdictions can thus share information on activists, helping them to anticipate and prepare for activist operations. The organizations' uses of the media become information for those who would control them. The attention they seek becomes a weapon to be used against them.

The Impact of the Anti-Abortion Movement on Social Change and Technological Development

The relationship between the anti-abortion movement and social change has not been unidirectional. The movement has had a definitive impact on social and technological change, largely through the offices of presidents Reagan and Bush. For example, RU-486 was banned from importation into the United States, even though its effectiveness as an abortifacient that sidestepped some of the potential complications of a surgical abortion had been established in Europe. RU-486 was considered a potential treatment for conditions other than abortion, including breast cancer, brain tumors, Cushing's syndrome, AIDS, and endometriosis (one cause of infertility), and for the inducement of labor to reduce the need for Caesarian sections (Wickenden 1990). Research into those uses was impeded by the presidential ban.

The use of fetal tissue is another area in which the anti-abortion movement has impeded medical research—in this case influencing the Reagan administration to institute a ban on its importation and utilization and the Bush administration to uphold the ban, which was limited to those researchers using federal funds. The most promising research on fetal tissue "involves the use of fetal brain, pancreas and liver tissue to treat Parkinson's disease, Huntington's chorea, spinal chord injuries, diabetes, leukemia, aplastic anemia and radiation sickness" (*New York Times,* 16 August 1987).[7]

The anti-abortion movement has consistently opposed in vitro fertilization, artificial insemination, and the use of surrogate mothers, as discussed in chapter 4. It even opposes the process when both the sperm and egg are from a married couple and it is the wife who is inseminated or implanted with a fertilized egg. Reagan directives forbade the use of federal funds in any of these efforts to induce fertility, a policy continued by George Bush. At first glance, this opposition appears contradictory to the "pro-family" stance of the movement. But both the Catholic and Protestant wings of the movement seem to subscribe the natural law theory cited above, which objects to all artificial means of both obviating and assisting pregnancies.

Thus, the movement has had a significant effect on the development of medical treatment and technology. It has also curtailed efforts to limit world population growth. Paradoxically, it has also circumscribed efforts of infertile couples seeking to have children.

Chapter 9

Framing the Future
of the Abortion Debate

This concluding chapter briefly assesses the anti-abortion move-ment's accomplishments to date and—based on these accomplish-ments and the general reluctance of the American public to fall hard on one side of the issue or the other—charts a likely course for the abortion debate in years to come.

The Movement to Date

The Legacy of the Webster and Pennsylvania Decisions
Following the 3 July 1989 *Webster* decision, in which the Supreme Court made allowances for states to regulate abortions while at the same time technically preserving the 1973 decisions in *Roe* and *Doe,* a number of states moved quickly to enact restrictive legislation. These various state acts included disallowance of abortions in any facility or hospital receiving public funds; requirement of a waiting period, usu-ally 24 hours, between seeking and receiving an abortion; require-ment of physicians to inform patients of fetal development; and requirement of notification, and sometimes approval, of the spouse, father, or parents, sometimes both, prior to an abortion. Some states and territories even passed laws forbidding abortions in virtually any instance, including rape, incest, or danger to the woman's life, in hopes of completely overturning *Roe* and *Doe.*

On 29 June 1992 the Supreme Court rendered its decision in *Planned Parenthood of Southeastern Pennsylvania v. Casey*, popularly known as the Pennsylvania case. The Pennsylvania provisions were an outgrowth of the *Webster* decision. While striking down the requirement that a woman must inform her husband that she was seeking an abortion and technically and explicitly reaffirming the *Roe* and *Doe* decisions in asserting that states could not ban most abortions, the Court, according to many analysts, severely restricted those decisions. It upheld the right of Pennsylvania to require physicians to inform women seeking abortions about fetal development and alternatives to abortion; to require women to wait 24 hours after getting that information before actually getting an abortion; to require physicians to keep detailed records of each abortion performed—records subject to public disclosure; and to require unmarried females under 18 and not self-supporting to get the permission of a parent or of a judge who has determined that the girl is mature enough to make her own decision.

While both sides of the dispute decried the decision, the Supreme Court essentially attempted to take a middle ground (Kaplan and Cohn 1992). At the same time, the restrictions it accepted severely limit access to abortion, particularly for poor women who would have difficulty making two trips to a clinic and for minors who might have abusive parents. Also, the potential for the public disclosure of physician records appears to violate the core of *Roe* and *Doe,* the right to privacy.

The Status of State Regulations   As of July 1992, 36 states had parental consent laws, 20 enforcing them. Twenty-six of those states allowed for judicial by-pass of parental consent; 10 had no such provision. Thirty states forbade use of Medicaid for the poor seeking abortions except when the woman's life was threatened. Twenty-six states mandated counseling concerning fetal development and alternatives to abortion. A waiting period, usually of one day, was required by 13 states (National Abortion Rights Action League and Alan Guttmacher Institute, cited in Salholz 1992).

Laws forbidding abortion, usually except in extreme cases, such as danger to the mother's life, rape, and incest, remain on many states' books, even though *Roe* and *Doe* made them unenforceable. Several states have enacted or re-enacted such laws since *Roe* and *Doe*. Many recently passed state laws, especially following the *Webster* decision, by restricting access to abortion, criminalize nonallowable abortions. Interestingly, the vast majority of these laws criminalize only the performance of abortions, not the act of having one. That is, the woman getting an abortion would not be violating the law, while the person providing her with the service would. This is comparable with making prostitution, but not the solicitation of prostitution, illegal.

Why would legislators be so selective in defining the criminal in the act of abortion when similar definitions are not generally applied to illegal betting, prostitution, moonshine liquor, illegal drugs, and other so-called "victimless" crimes? For one thing, the majority of the women seeking abortions today are young and single. While the general public does not support abortion as a birth control technique, it does have sympathy for the young unwed mother. On the other hand, the abortion provider, both legal and illegal, has been characterized by the anti-abortion movement as operating solely out of a profit motive and taking advantage of women caught in moral and social dilemmas. That is, the woman tends to be viewed as a victim, the abortionist as a villain. Thus, legislators have generally concluded that they could secure greater public support for limitations that criminalized the performance of abortions without punishing the purchaser of the service.

Progress, of Sorts, for the Movement   The American people are clearly divided over the issue of abortion (Dionne 1989c). While they strongly support the option of abortion in "difficult" cases, such as danger to the woman's life, incest, rape, and a severely impaired fetus, they also tend to oppose it as a means of birth control or sex selection. On the other hand, the use of abortion when birth control fails, when a woman who thought she could no longer conceive suddenly discovers she is pregnant, or when a 12- or 13-year-old gets pregnant are more nebulous questions the polls seldom, if ever, probe. Furthermore, while many Americans are uncomfortable with the availability of abortion, they remain strongly opposed to government interference in our personal lives.

Realizing that their all-or-nothing position is held by a small minority, many in the anti-abortion movement are willing to accept limited restrictions on the general availability of abortion in the hope that these restrictions will pave the way for an eventual all-out ban. The treasurer of the National Right to Life Committee, Roger Mall, indicated "that while his side hoped for an outright ban on abortion someday, it knew it would have to settle for less now. 'We're willing to save as much as we can, as soon as we can'" (Dionne 1989c).

One tactic of some elements in the movement is to present the opposition as extremist. As David Carlin, majority leader of the Rhode Island Senate, said, "When you're dealing with the mushy middle, the more extreme you can make your opponent look, the better off you are" (Dionne 1989c). The anti-abortion movement has a particular problem in this regard: a *New York Times*/CBS News poll in 1989 revealed that 44 percent of those polled viewed anti-abortionists as extremists, while only 33 percent looked upon supporters of abortion rights as extreme.

That perception of the extremism of the anti-abortion movement has been heightened since 1989 by the activities of groups such as Operation Rescue, the Lambs for Christ, and Missionaries to the Pre-Born. While I am not aware of any poll since 1989 probing the public's perceptions of the extremism of the opposing groups, the pro-choice groups have concentrated in that period on legal attacks and on defensive escort services that protect women from hostile clinic demonstrators. These tactics are less confrontational and more acceptable to the "law and order" middle in the United States. I would suggest, therefore, that the general perception of the anti-abortion movement as extremist is likely to have increased since 1989.

In addition, the *Webster* and Pennsylvania decisions of the Supreme Court have placed adherents of the pro-choice movement in a defensive, besieged position, potentially garnering a degree of sympathy for them and their cause, since those decisions heighten government control of what are perceived as personal decisions. As early as 1989, however, organizations in the pro-choice movement began using media consultants and stressing appeals to the "mushy middle's" wariness of government control over individual lives and choices, a typically conservative value (Dionne 1989a).

In some ways not generally recognized the anti-abortion movement has been quite effective. Fewer physicians are being trained to perform abortions; while about 25 percent of the medical schools offered training in first and second trimesters in 1985, by 1991 only 12 percent did so for the first trimester and 7 percent for the second. The number of physicians performing abortions has also decreased. Contributing to the decline are the low status within the profession of those performing abortions; the risk of intimidation and harassment, including threats to physicians and their families, demonstrations, and the arson and bombing of clinics; the relatively low income compared with other specializations; and the legal roadblocks hampering the opening of clinics (Lacayo 1992).

Furthermore, hospitals have been retreating from performing abortions. In the decade following *Roe* and *Doe* hospitals performed about half the abortions, while now they conduct about 10 percent of them (Lacayo 1992). For one thing, the large number of clinics that arose could perform abortions at a much lower cost than could hospitals. For another, many hospitals opted out of offering abortions because of directors or donors that were against it. As mentioned previously, the clinics where most abortions are now performed have the disadvantage of being more accessible to demonstrators, arsonists, and bombers, because of their location and their general lack of security services. The physicians and other personnel working in them are also more easily targeted (Lacayo 1992). Thus, a number of clinics have closed. Also, as mentioned previously, the vast majority of clinics are located in urban areas, making abortion difficult to access for most women in small towns and rural areas. North Dakota has one clinic in the state, Mississippi three, all in Jackson.

Other barriers to the availability of abortion include parental notification, the 24-hour waiting period, the unavailability of Medicaid financing, requirements that clinics have advance transfer agreements with hospitals for clients who might suffer complications from an abortion, and prohibitions against publicly financed facilities or public employees performing abortions or counseling women about the availability of abortion. Some states may in the future attempt to require clinics to have the same equipment that hospitals have, which would increase costs.

In sum, the anti-abortion movement and its sympathizers have been quite effective in making abortions more difficult to secure, especially for women in lower income groups.

The Future of the Movement

Anything I can say about the future of the anti-abortion movement is speculation. The stage on which the movement must play out its agenda is being determined by forces outside of its control. For example, although the Reagan-Bush appointments to the Supreme Court have had the effect of limiting access to abortion, the election of Bill Clinton and his pledge to use *Roe v. Wade* as a litmus test for Supreme Court appointments could turn things around. Furthermore, a Democratic administration could result in much stronger sanctions against groups such as Operation Rescue. In 1992 a largely Democratic Congress passed a freedom of choice bill before the Republican convention, which President Bush vetoed, emphasizing the differences between the Republican and Democratic parties before the November elections. Thus, national circumstances may well continue to determine the options open to the movement.

Effects of Supreme Court Appointments   While the Reagan-Bush appointments to the Supreme Court have resulted in restrictions on the access to abortion, they clearly have not fulfilled the hopes of the anti-abortion movement, nor have they likely fulfilled the hopes of those presidents. Political pundits are still surprised by the divisions within the Court on certain issues. While limiting access to abortion, the Court has also banned prayers at public school graduation ceremonies and accepted flag burning. On the other hand, those appointments and the Court's *Webster* and Pennsylvania decisions have placed the pro-choice movement on the defensive and motivated its adherents to greater mobilization. The history of social movements in general teaches us that fairly strong movements do not suffer from tough government sanctions but rather become stronger when on the defensive. Thus, the Court has had the effect of revitalizing the pro-choice movement.

The disappointment expressed by the anti-abortion movement with the Court decisions may be in part a public relations effort aimed at maintaining the motivation and activism of its constituencies. Whatever the movement's responses, the general public more likely views the decisions as anti-abortion victories, although limited ones. Thus, the decisions will probably weaken the movement or at bring about a decline or a slowing of the increase in the numbers of its activists. Because the Court decisions reflect to a degree the ill-defined sentiments of America's "mushy middle"—if not going beyond those sentiments in terms of restrictiveness—the public is likely to view the disruptive tactics of Operation Rescue, Lambs for Christ, and similar groups as much less warranted. Support for negative political sanctions against these groups and their leaders will likely rise. And the willingness of public officials to apply such sanctions will accordingly likely increase, especially under a Democratic administration.

Effects of RICO and "Ku Klux Klan" Laws   The application of the Racketeer Influenced Corrupt Organizations and "Ku Klux Klan" laws to those who would limit access to abortion clinics are at this writing undergoing appeals. Meanwhile, the number of such cases grows, and the fines imposed by lower courts continue to grow as well. Organizational funds have been seized and frozen, as have, and probably will be even more, those of the stand-in groups that have arisen to replace them. Under some court rulings, their funds could even be turned over to the groups they oppose. Meanwhile, significant amounts of funds, time, energy, and personnel must be devoted to legal defenses, further diverting the resources of the movement organizations involved. While some organizations have attempted to turn these court cases into media events and rites of intensification, such efforts have largely failed. For example, Randall Terry tried to turn a California trial into a massive public relations event, but he was able to gather only a couple of dozen supporters (Faux 1990). RICO and conspiracy laws have the potential of breaking the back of those organizations using tactics that obstruct access to legal businesses.

If that should happen, it is likely that the movement organizations using more traditional tactics, such as lobbying and supporting candidates for political office, will gain greater prominence. They could also gain supporters from the more radical groups, who would try to move the more traditional organizations toward a greater degree of activism. Thus, those groups which now find picketing undesirable might find in the future that they have identified members doing such in their name. Such an organization, rather than growing more radical overall, could develop internal divisions and disputes that would be disruptive and debilitating. In sum, developments within the less radical organizations are problematical and depend on developments now largely outside their control.

On the other hand, the success of RICO suits could drive the more radical activists underground and toward more radical behavior. It is likely that at least some of the more focused and committed among them could move toward greater violence, resulting in heightened waves of bombings and arsons of clinics. From my previous research, I predict this as a more likely result than the tempering of the movement. Half the bombers and arsonists tried and convicted for those acts had previously participated in "peaceful" demonstrations and picketing and became frustrated with what they perceived as the ineffectiveness of such tactics (Blanchard and Prewitt 1993).

Effects of RU-486: Reprivatization of Abortion   Given the American experience with prohibition, gambling, prostitution, and illegal drugs, it is highly unlikely that RU-486 will long be withheld from women who want to use it as an abortifacient. If those who specialize in supplying illegal goods and services to a desiring public do not enter soon into the illegal importation trade of RU-486, feminist groups will. As mentioned earlier in this volume, there already exist groups helping women to find access to abortions in states where limitations have been or are expected to be placed on them. There are also cadres training women in self-abortion. These existing groups could easily turn their ingenuity and efforts toward methods of importing and distributing RU-486. The ability of such groups to function with impunity prior to *Roe* and *Doe* points to their likelihood of success with RU-486.

It is also likely that assistance in these efforts will come from elements within the medical community. It is unlikely that nurses and physicians will idly observe the complete loss of legal abortions and the drastic increase in medical complications and deaths from illegal abortions, given their behavior prior to 1973. Thus, given the cooperation that arose between some physicians and feminists before 1973, as in the groups Clergymen's Consultation and Jane, it is most likely that such coalitions would rise again. RU-486 would provide a much easier and less detectable method for evading those restrictions than did the surgical procedures available prior to *Roe* and *Doe*.

Effects of More Restrictions on the Accessibility of Abortion
Now that an entire generation of women has grown up under liberalized abortion laws, it is highly unlikely that the outlawing or placing of severe restrictions on abortion availability will be effective. Likewise, the improvements in medical technology since 1973 virtually ordain that the availability of safe abortions—even if through illegal, underground networks or self-abortion—will not and cannot be significantly reversed, particularly for middle- and upper-class women. It is axiomatic that life choices are determined by social class and, in the case of abortion, by geographical location.[1] Thus, working- and lower-class, young, and rural females would most likely go back to utilizing more dangerous methods of abortion—illegal abortionists in unsanitary circumstances or, more likely, self-induced methods that are life-threatening. The resulting increase in emergency hospital admissions from botched abortions and the associated rise in the female death rate would likely create a backlash against abortion restrictions.

Furthermore, feminist groups, particularly NOW chapters, promise acts of civil disobedience to protest abortion restrictions. Between the *Webster* and Pennsylvania decisions, local chapters published materials on the nature of civil disobedience.[2] Abortion will remain a public, disruptive issue, likely to be stirred up by one side or the other.

Effects of the Clinton Administration   The effects of Bill Clinton's election in 1992 may well be far-reaching. On the twentieth anniversary of *Roe* and *Doe,* while the annual March for Life was in progress in Washington, D.C., Clinton rescinded the Bush limitations on funding organizations that advised pregnant women of abortion as an option, directed regulators to reassess the ban on importation of RU-486, permitted abortions at overseas military hospitals at the patient's expense, promised to restore funding to U.N. health organizations dealing with international birth control, and removed the ban on federal financing of fetal tissue research. During his campaign he pledged to sign a legislative act establishing *Roe* and *Doe* provisions as the law of the land.

It is likely that the role of the Justice Department in court cases will shift from *amicus curiae* support for anti-abortion groups to support for abortion supporters. The role of the FBI and other federal agencies in investigating and prosecuting anti-abortion organizations such as Operation Rescue is also expected to shift to the pro-choice side. A number of those efforts should be made easier with the concurrent election of more women and Democrats to the Congress. (See, for example, Price 1992.) Additional changes might include the use of federal funds for abortions by the poor. Of even greater long-term effect is likely to be Clinton's appointments to the Supreme Court; his first, Ruth Bader Ginsburg, newly sworn in to office as this book went to press, is supportive of choice for women.

The Clinton election represents a basic shift in federal weight and power in the abortion debate. It will recast not only the legal support for the anti-abortion movement but also the aura of legitimacy surrounding it. A siege mentality could, and likely would, descend on the movement, revitalizing it, since it will be placed on the defensive. After initial revitalization to achieve its goals in federal regulations and laws, the pro-choice movement will likely undergo a gradual decline in its organizations' membership.[3]

Conclusions

In 1986 Martin Durham indicated the need for research on divisions in the anti-abortion movement and its relations to the New Right, on relations between men and women in the movement, and on the reasons why evangelicals had become involved in a traditionally Catholic movement. Since Durham's challenge, these questions have been largely answered.

First, it has been well established that the New Right helped to influence the anti-abortion movement for its own political purposes, primarily to put Ronald Reagan and George Bush in office. The resources of the New Right—political knowledge, mailing lists, and financial resources—allowed the movement to reach and motivate people who might not otherwise have been enlisted.

Second, it has become increasingly clear that men dominate the leadership of the movement, most especially among the more radical groups. Women are used more as foot soldiers, filling traditionally feminine roles as they performing secretarial and other routine tasks. Thus, the male superiority ideology of the movement is reflected in who assigns and performs its tasks. When females lead organizations, they are usually charismatic figures, such as Judie Brown, who resemble the female charismatic leaders in the Pentecostal/Charismatic religious movements and are marked by their rarity.

Third, the evangelicals in the movement are primarily fundamentalists who act out of defense of their conceptions of male/female roles and their desire to reinstitute the medieval hegemony of religion over other social institutions, particularly the law (Blanchard and Prewitt 1993). Some Catholic groups appear to operate from a similar perspective.

The anti-abortion movement in general is a movement of cultural fundamentalism, seeking to reestablish "traditional" male-female relationships, particularly the dependence of females on males and their ability to hold males responsible for their sexual behavior and for their fathering roles. It transcends religions and forges a common bond between cultural and religious fundamentalists across religious groups and perspectives that are at odds on a large number of other issues. The common bond is their definition of husband-wife, male-female, parent-child positions of dominance and authority versus obedience and submission.

Appendix: Major Publications and Organizations of the Anti-Abortion Movement

The publications and organizations of the movement wax and wane. To the best of my knowledge, these organizations and publications are extant as of the date of this publication.

Organizations

Ad Hoc Committee in Defense of Life, 810 National Press Building, 529 14th Street, Washington, DC 20045.

Advocates for Life Ministries, P. O. Box 13656, Portland, OR 97213. (*International Life Advocate.*)

The African-American Society against Abortion, 5724 40th Avenue South, Minneapolis, MN 55417.

American Association of Pro Life Obstetricians and Gynecologists, 266 Pine Avenue, Lauderdale-by-the-Sea, FL 33308.

American Association of Pro Life Pediatricians, 2160 S. First Avenue, Maywood, IL 60153.

American Catholic Lay Network, 3017 4th Street NE, Washington, DC 20017.

American Citizens Concerned for Life, 6127 Excelsior Blvd., Minneapolis, MN 55416.

American Life League, P. O. Box 1350, Stafford, VA 22554. (*ALL About Issues.*)

American Life Lobby, Inc., P. O. Box 490, Stafford, VA 22554.

Americans against Abortion, 6728 E. 13th Street, Tulsa, OK 74112. (Some sources list P.O. Box 40, Lindale, TX 75771, the same address as Last Days Ministries.)

Americans United for Life, 343 S. Dearborn Street, Chicago, IL 60604.

Arthur S. DeMoss Foundation, P. O. Box 700, Valley Forge, PA 19482-0700.

Association of Black Catholics against Abortion, 1011 First Avenue, New York, NY 10022.

Baptists for Life, P. O. Box 394, Hallettsville, TX 77964.

Birthright, USA, 686 N. Broad Street, Woodbury, NJ 08096. (*Life Guardian.*)

Carriage House, 418 C Street NE, Washington, DC 20002.

Catholic Life & Family Center, Box 7244, Collegeville, MN 56321. *(Life & Family News.)*

Catholics United for Life, 3050 Gap Knob Road, New Hope, KY 40052. (*Youth Crusader News.*)

Christian Action Council, 101 West Broad, Suite 500, Falls Church, VA 22046-4200. (*Pro-Life Advocate.*)

Christian Life Commission of the Southern Baptist Convention, 901 Commerce Street, Suite 550, Nashville, TN 37203.

Comite Pro-Vida, P. O. Box 150704, Miami, FL 33165.

Committee to Protect the Family Foundation, 8001 Forbes Place, Suite 102, Springfield, VA 22151.

Concerned Women for America, 370 L'Enfant Promenade SW, Suite 800, Washington, DC 20024.

Dads for Life, 908 Thorn Street, Princeton, WV 24740.

Democrats for Life, 1711 Bopp Road, St. Louis, MO 63131.

Doctors for Life, 11511 Trivoli Lane, St. Louis, MO 63141.

Eagle Forum, P. O. Box 618, Alton, IL 62002.

Evangelicals for Social Action, P. O. Box 76560, Washington, DC 20013, or 712 G Street SE, Washington, DC 20003.

Fathers for Life, Father's Rights Legal Services, 3623 Douglas Avenue, Des Moines, IA 50310.

Feminists for Life of America, 811 E. 47th Street, Kansas City, MO 64110. (*Sisterlife.*)

Focus on the Family, 801 Corporate Center Drive, Pomona, CA 91764.

Forlife, P.O. Drawer 1279, Tryon, NC 28782.

Friends for Life, 18 North Michigan Avenue, Chicago, IL 60601.

Heart Light, P. O. Box 8513. Green Bay, WI 54308.

Human Life Center, St. John's University, Collegeville, MN 56321.

Human Life Foundation, 150 East 35th Street, New York, NY 10016.

Human Life International, 7845 Airpark Road, Suite E, Gaithersburg, MD 20879. (*Human Life Review.*)

Jewish Anti-Abortion League, 1821 Ocean Parkway, Brooklyn, NY 11223.

JustLife, P. O. Box 15263, Washington, DC 20003. (*JustLife.*)

Lambs of Christ, P. O. Box 43333, Las Vegas, NV 89116. (*The Gathering . . . of the Lambs.*)

Last Days Ministries. P.O. Box 40, Lindale, TX 75771-0040.

Libertarians for Life, 13424 Hathaway Drive, Wheaton, MD 20906.

Liberty Federation, 505 Second Street NE, Washington, DC 20002.

Life Amendment Political Action Committee, P. O. Box 14236, Ben Franklin Station, Washington, DC 20044.

Life Chain, 3209 Colusa Highway, Yuba City, CA 95993.

Life-PAC, 310 Sixth Street SE, Washington, DC 20003.

Lutherans for Life, P. O. Box 819, Benton, AR 72015, or 275 N Syndicate, St. Paul, MN 55104.

March for Life, Box 2950, Washington, DC 20003.

Missionaries to the Preborn, P. O. Box 25204, Milwaukee, WI 53277. (*Life Advocate.*)

Missionaries to the Preborn-Atlanta, 1033 Franklin Road, #297, Marietta, GA 30067.

Missionaries to the Preborn-Wichita, P. O. Box 20915, Wichita, KS 67208.

National Association of Pro-Life Nurses, P. O. Box 64, Elysian, MN 56028. (*Pulse-Line.*)

National Committee for a Human Life Amendment, 1707 L Street NW, Suite 400, Washington, DC 20036.

National Organization of Episcopalians for Life, 10523 Main Street, Suite 35, Fairfax, VA 22030.

National Right to Life Committee, 419 7th Street NW, Suite 500, Washington, DC 20004. (*National Right to Life News.*)

Nurses for Life, P. O. Box 4818, Detroit, MI 48219.

O.M.E.G.A., P. O. Box 11796, Ft. Lauderdale, FL 33306.

Operation Rescue, P. O. Box 1180, Binghampton, NY 13902. (Officially replaced by Lampstand Ministries in 1990; address unchanged.)

Operation Rescue-Florida, Melbourne, FL. (*Florida Rescuer.*)

Operation Rescue National, P. O. Box 127, Sommerville, SC 29484.

Orthodox Christians for Life, P. O. Box 805, Melville, NY 11747.

Pearson Foundation, 36633 Lindell Boulevard, Suite 290, St. Louis, MO 63108.

Presbyterians Pro-Life-Research, Education and Care, Inc., P. O. Box 19290, Minneapolis, MN 55419.

Pro-Life Action League, 6160 N Cicero, #600, Chicago, IL 60646. (*Direct Action News.*)

Pro-Life Action Ministries, 1163 Payne, St. Paul, MN 55101.

Pro-Life Action Network, 6160 N Cicero, #600, Chicago, IL 60646. (*Action News.*)

Pro-Life Direct Action League, P. O. Box 11881, St. Louis, MO 63105.

Pro-Life Nonviolent Action Project, P. O. Box 2193, Gaithersburg, MD 20879.

Prolifers for Survival, 1215 Quincy Street, Washington, DC 20017-2635.

Public Health Workers for Life, P. O. Box 57411, Washington, DC 20037.

Religious Roundtable, 1500 Wilson Boulevard, Arlington, VA 22209.

Rescue America, Box 7290257-220, Houston, TX 77272.

Rescue America of Florida, Inc., P. O. Box 608256, Orlando, FL 32860-8256, or 2000 NE 51st Place, Ocala, FL 32670.

The Rutherford Institute, P. O. Box 510, Manassas, VA 22110.

The Seamless Garment Network, Jefferson City, MO.

Task Force of United Methodists on Abortion and Sexuality, c/o Ruth Brown, Director, 512 Florence Street, Dothan, AL 36301.

Ultramentane Associates, Inc., 206 Marquette Avenue, South Bend, IN 46617. (*Fidelity.*)

United Church of Christ Friends for Life, RD 1, Box 366, Bechtelsville, PA 19505.

U.S. Coalition for Life, P.O. Box 315, Export, PA 15632. (*Pro-Life Legislative Services, Pro-Life Reporter.*)

Value of Life Committee, 637 Cambridge Street, Brighton, MA 02135.

Women Exploited by Abortion (WEBA), 1553 24th Street, Des Moines, IA 50311.

Youth Organizations

American Collegians for Life, P. O. Box 1112, Washington, DC 20013.

College Pro-Life Information Network, P. O. Box 10664, State College, PA 16805.

National Teens for Life, 419 Seventh Street NW, Suite 500, Washington, DC 20004-2293.

National Youth Pro-Life Committee, P. O. Box 67, Newport, KY 41071.

Youth for America (an arm of Missionaries to the Preborn), 1033 Franklin Road, Suite 297, Marietta, GA 30067.

Legal Services

American Family Association Law Center, Tupelo, MS.

Free Speech Advocates, 3050 Knob Gap Road, New Hope, KY 40062.

"Service" Organizations

Alternatives to Abortion International, Hillcrest Hotel, Suite 511, Toledo, OH 43699, or 46 N Broadway, Yonkers, NY 10701. (*Heartbeat.*)

Birthright, 686 North Broad Street, Woodbury, NJ 08096.

Liberty Godparent Ministry, P. O. Box 27000, Lynchburg, VA 24506.

Several Sources Foundation, P. O. Box 157, Ramsey, NJ 07446.

Sexual Assault Pregnancy Support

Fortress, P. O. Box 7352, Springfield, IL 62791.

Life after Assault League, 1336 West Lindbergh, Appleton, WI 54914.

Post-Abortion Counseling

After Abortion Helpline, 21 Violet Street, Providence, RI 02908.

American Victims of Abortion, 419 Seventh Street NW, Suite 402, Washington, DC 10004-2293. (A National Right to Life Committee organization.)

Institute for Abortion Recovery and Research, 111 Bow Street, Portsmouth, NH 03801-3819.

National Office of Post-Abortion Reconciliation and Healing, 3501 South Lake Drive, P. O. Box 07477, Milwaukee, WI 53207-0477.

Open ARMS, P. O. Box 1056, Columbia, MO 65205.

Post Abortion Counseling and Education, 101 West Broad Street, Suite 500, Falls Church, VA 22046. (Affiliated with the Christian Action Council.)

Project Rachel, c/o Respect for Life Office, Archdiocese of Milwaukee, P. O. Box 2018, Milwaukee, WI 53201.

Victims of Choice, P. O. Box 6268, Vacaville, CA 95696-6268.

Women Exploited by Abortion (WEBA), Route 1, Box 821, Venus, TX 76084.

Materials and Resources

American Portrait Films/Reel to Reel Productions, P. O. Box 19266-44119, Cleveland, OH 44119.

Bernadell, Inc., P. O. Box 1897, Old Chelsea Station, New York, NY 10113-0950.

Hayes Publishing Company, 6304 Hamilton Avenue, Cincinnati, OH 45224.

Heritage House, P. O. Box 730, Taylor, AZ 85939.

International Life Services, 2606 1/2 West Eighth Street, Los Angeles, CA 90057. (*Living Word.*)

Right to Life Education Committee, 2340 Porter Street, P. O. Box 901, Grand Rapids, MI 49509.

Notes

Chapter 1

1. The section of "A Note on Terminology" is taken virtually verbatim from Blanchard and Prewitt (1993).

2. Kelly (1991) distinguishes the terms *anti-abortion, right to life,* and *pro-life* and equates the pro-life position with a broader, consistent ethic that would include social and economic justice for women, attacking what he perceives as underlying reasons for women to seek abortions in the first place.

3. Even some proponents of the anti-abortion movement refer to it as such. See Hentoff 1989.

4. Right-wing strategist Paul Weyrich said, "Some of the pro-life movement definitely feels that the Administration has given them rhetoric but not action" (*New York Times,* 26 January 1987). Spitzer (1987:67) asserts, "Many in the right-to-life movement continue to voice dissatisfaction with candidates like . . . Ronald Reagan. Even enthusiastic Reagan supporters in the RTLP view Reagan with suspicion and cynicism, calculating that his sympathies are founded in political expediency more than ideological fervor."

Chapter 2

1. This summary of Roman Catholic positions is based on Noonan (1967, 1968).

2. Some Catholic theologians even believed they could distinguish the sex of a fetus and maintained that it took females twice as long as males to be ensouled (80 days versus 40 days); when the sex of a fetus could not be "determined," the fetus was assumed to be female (Huser 1942:18).

3. This discussion of the legal and medical history of abortion in the United States is based primarily on Mohr (1978).

4. Keown (1985) finds a parallel development in England at about the same time.

5. Caron (1989) concludes that this fear of higher birthrates among immigrants and the lower classes persisted into the 1960s and led to support for birth control and sterilization for those classes.

6. For a feminist examination of some of the following trends as they apply in the twentieth century see Petchesky (1984).

7. Another force behind the push for public education was to initiate non-Anglo Saxon immigrants into American language and culture; that is, to negate "foreign" influences.

8. It is not coincidental that while these changes were taking place religious fundamentalism began to arise, in about 1880. It has been established that fundamentalism is basically a reaction against modernization (see, for example, Blanchard and Prewitt 1992) and a primary force in the anti-abortion movement.

9. The "quality of life" issue is at least partially a spin-off of the increased valuation of health in American life since the 1870s. With the discovery of anesthesia at about the time of the Civil War, the beginnings of the public health movement early in the twentieth century, and the increasing control over of communicable diseases, health (wholeness) became for the first time defined as an element in the basic standard of living.

10. Among some extreme racists, prohibition of abortion was seen as a means of preventing white Anglo-Saxon women from having sexual relations with African-American men. If abortion were available to them, they could remove evidence of illicit relations.

11. While the AMA estimates that about 5 percent of American physicians are incompetent, fewer than 100 physicians lose their licenses each year. More than that many attorneys are disbarred annually in the state of Florida.

12. Luker (1984:53) estimates that in the early twentieth century there were a minimum 14 illegal abortions for every licit one.

13. Induced abortions are, however, sent to a laboratory for analysis to make sure that cancer or other abnormalities are not present. These remains are disposed of by the laboratories in accordance with state laws.

14. The latest death rates I could obtain, from the Alan Guttmacher Institute in Washington, D.C., are (1) from abortion, 0.5 per 100,000, and (2) from birth, 12–18 per 100,000.

15. See, for example, Volpe (1984). Recent developments in genetic engineering to combat genetic deformities promise a much more broadened role of the fetus as patient.

16. As Luker (1984) points out, this concept of the developmental stages of the fetus parallels that of the nineteenth-century—that abortion in the early development of the fetus is comparable to birth control.

17. At this writing, some fetuses are viable at 21 weeks, about 5 weeks short of the third trimester. The most premature infants to survive were 18

weeks premature, and there were only two such cases (*Pensacola News Journal,* 25 July 1992:3A). On 12 December 1991, Cable News Network reported the introduction of a new surfactant that enhances the maturation of the lungs of premature babies, improving their survival rates by about 40 percent. Physicians working on other surfactants predict that by the year 2000 some fetuses will be able to survive at 18 weeks, about halfway through the normal gestation period.

18. Studies of "feral" and socially isolated children have shown the extreme importance of social interaction in human development. The vast majority of children deprived of human interaction in their early years die by the time of their mid- or late-teens, despite medical and psychological intervention.

19. The vast majority of state laws forbidding or regulating abortion, both before and after 1973, made those performing abortions, physicians and nonphysicians, criminally responsible, but exempted the woman from criminal prosecution. This is the only "crime," to my knowledge, in which the conscious initiator of it is immune from prosecution.

20. As Luker (1984) indicates, there was among medical practitioners, as there still is, a wide range of belief about the circumstances under which abortion is acceptable. Furthermore, many physicians were allowing extremely deformed neonatals to die at birth from a lack of attention. For evidence of the frequency of "illegal" abortions prior to 1973 see Gold *et al.* (1965) and Hall (1965a, 1965b, 1967a, 1967b).

21. In 1992 the Overground Railroad, a Pennsylvania organization, became publicly known as an organization ready to assist women seeking legal abortions should the Pennsylvania limits on abortions be accepted by the Supreme Court; it is a revitalization of the pre-Roe organization of the same name.

22. Formal organizations include the National Abortion Rights Action League (NARAL, 1969; formerly the National Association for the Repeal of Abortion Laws); Zero Population Growth (ZPG, 1968); the National Organization for Women (NOW, 1969); the Abortion Rights Association; Abortion Rights Mobilization; the Wisconsin Committee to Legalize Abortion (circa 1966); and the National Abortion Federation (NAF). Of course, all of these were preceded by the Planned Parenthood, founded by Margaret Sanger in 1922 as the Birth Control League of America to promote birth control and only later picked up on the abortion issue. See also chapter 3.

23. At the turn of the century a woman could expect, with the higher birth rate, early marriage, and higher female death rate, to have only about one year of life left after her last child left home. By the 1980s she would have closer to 30 or more years of life left, as well as a longer period before having the first child. Contributing to women's increased longevity was development

of antibiotics during and following World War II, which led to a dramatic decrease in the maternal death rate.

24. The increased valuation and general acceptance of the right of women to choose to bear or not bear children is indicated by a 1992 World Health Organization report on contraception, which states, in part, "Without fertility regulation, women's rights are mere words. A woman who has no control over her fertility cannot complete her education, cannot maintain gainful employment . . . and has very few real choices open to her" (*Pensacola News Journal,* 25 June 1992).

25. The differences in women's valuations of men may be characterized as a difference between extrinsic and intrinsic valuations; between what the man can offer a woman in the way of meeting other goals and what the man is in and of himself.

26. The population explosion is primarily the result of a drastically reduced rate of death without a concomitant reduction in birth rates, mostly in Third World nations in Asia, Africa, and Latin America.

Chapter 3

1. Estimates indicate that as many as 20,000 deformed and handicapped infants were born as a result of the 1964 German measles epidemic (Petchesky 1984).

2. For a description of the Service and an explanation of its success, see Bart 1987. Fascinating is her conclusion that the most important factor in the organization's success was lack of concern for its own survival.

3. The do-it-yourself part of the movement reflects the growing health movement, one aspect of which is the demedicalization and deprofessionalization of health care; that is, Americans are increasingly taking control of their own health from physicians, who have continued for almost a century to claim that they were the final arbiters of health and treatment. See, for example, Goldstein (1992). Another aspect of the movement is to assume personal control over one's death.

To contact the Service, women were given a telephone number and told to ask for Jane. The Service may be rising again. In June 1990 250 persons attending the annual meeting of the National Women's Studies Association had four former members of the Service tell them how to run such an illegal operation (Blakely 1990:78).

4. In another research effort (Blanchard and Prewitt 1992) the author contacted every clinic that had been the victim of arson, bombing, or other extreme violence prior to 1991. A representative of *every* such clinic reported that at least one former picketer had later come seeking an abortion for herself or her teenage daughter. The ex-picketer's opening statement was always virtually the same, "I didn't realize . . . "

5. There were those who felt the effects of reform laws were still too restrictive. A Maryland physician, for example, asserted that the reform of that state's laws had a minimal effect on criminal abortions, for legal abortions were still virtually unavailable to the poor and many hospitals used quotas to restrict the number of abortions performed. While Maryland had the highest therapeutic abortion rate in the country, 43 per 1,000 live births in 1969, it was estimated that the actual abortion rate was about 200 per 1,000 live births, and illegal abortions remained the primary cause of maternal death (Irwin 1970:22).

6. The account of California's experience with abortion law reform is based on Luker (1984); the account of Hawaii's with repeal is based on Steinhoff and Diamond (1977).

7. In its pamphlets "Humanist Manifesto I" and "Humanist Manifesto II" (Buffalo: Prometheus Books, 1973) the American Humanist Association asserts its basic principle of the primacy of reason over religious faith. Some humanists are also religious, as exemplified by the Fellowship of Religious Humanists. The majority of one religious group, the Unitarian-Universalists, maintains that they are non-Christian humanists (Tapp 1973).

8. "Mainline" denominations are the traditionally dominant, and somewhat liberal, Protestant churches in the United States: examples are the Episcopal, United Methodist, Presbyterian churches, the United Church of Christ, and some Lutheran churches.

9. For a physician's argument for repeal, see Mietus (1967).

10. See Killian (1972) on the functions of radicalism in a social movement.

11. Father Drinan, a Catholic priest, served in the U.S. House of Representatives until Pope Paul II decided that priests could not hold elected office.

12. As a layperson and a nonpolitical office holder, Pearson is perhaps an example of the "conversion syndrome," which holds that the new convert to a religion oversubscribes to its values and beliefs to prove his or her faith. People who grow up in a particular religious group tend not to be concerned about the acceptance of their status and are more relaxed in their religious observances.

13. Robert Pearson went so far as to argue that if the fetus is not ensouled till birth, it would be better to let it be born and then kill it, so that it can have a soul and thereby have access to eternal life (Steinhoff and Diamond 1977:99).

14. "Morally, the [Roman Catholic] Church contends that the natural death of mother and child is a lesser evil than the death of the fetal life through abortion" (Lader 1966:95–96).

15. As Steinhoff and Diamond (1977) point out, the term *innocent* has at least three meanings: innocent as opposed to guilty; spiritually pure, religiously innocent, pure and god-given; and helpless.

16. Lader (1973:72) implies that the establishment of the Family Life Bureaus and the indictment of physicians are related. Those indicted were either physicians or clergy, who received support from professional colleagues and the press. The indictments thus backfired, resulting in positive press for those indicted and negative press for the Catholic church and the anti-abortion movement.

17. The right to privacy doctrine was later used by the Supreme Court in a number of its decisions on other matters. A number of states have explicit right to privacy provisions in their constitutions: Florida, California, Alaska, Montana, Arizona, and Hawaii. Washington, Louisiana, and South Carolina have clauses that have been interpreted as guaranteeing privacy (Lewis 1989). In 1989 the Florida State Supreme Court overturned a state law requiring parental notification as a violation of the state constitutional right to privacy.

Garfield (1984:9) maintains that "the right to privacy is actually two rights: the individual's right not to have certain matters disclosed to the public or government, and the right to independence in making important and personal decisions, such as those pertaining to marriage and procreation."

18. In 1973, when first declared legal, clinic abortions cost about $200, while illegal abortions cost a minimum of $1000 and as much as $2000. By 1992, the cost of clinic abortions had risen only to about $300, much lower than the increase in the cost of living over that period. Hospital abortions incur the costs of the use of operating rooms, anesthesiologists, and other requirements associated with major surgery. Hospital abortions, then, usually cost more than illegal abortions.

In 1993 a clinic abortion typically cost $275–300 and a hospital abortion $1500–2000 or more. Prior to 1973, illegal abortion costs varied widely, usually depending on the training and competence of the abortionist, but the typical cost was probably about $1000.

19. Abortion, however, is easily available for the most part only in moderate- and large-sized urban areas. One state, North Dakota, had only one clinic performing abortions in 1992, in Fargo. Only about one-third of obstetrician-gynecologists nationwide perform abortions or acknowledge that they do. Also, it appears that the majority of those physicians working through clinics are actually based in other communities, which makes them less susceptible to pressures in the communities where they perform abortions.

20. There is practically no way of accurately determining the rate of spontaneous abortions. No records are kept, since many, if not most, occur before a woman is even aware that she is pregnant or in the first eight weeks of pregnancy. It is estimated that as many as half of all pregnancies are spontaneously aborted. (From interviews with obstetricians.)

21. "Four out of 10 pregnant black women in 1977 obtained abortions, compared to one of four pregnant white women" (Jaffe *et al.* 1981:11).

22. Numerous studies have shown that there is a strong prohibition against sexual intercourse for single women in the working class. While working-class males tend to measure their masculinity by their sexual prowess, working-class females are likely to feel that premarital sex is immoral. Consequently, working-class females often believe that planning for sexual intercourse—a requirement for the use of female contraceptives, be they birth control pills or diaphragms—is immoral. To plan ahead requires visiting a physician, going to a pharmacist to secure the prescription, then taking a pill daily or inserting the diaphragm prior to intercourse. It is viewed as less immoral to be overcome by passion in the heat of the moment. (See Farley 1987:214–15.) Additional deterrents to lower- and working-class teenage females using birth control lie in (1) their lower educational attainment, resulting in their not being as likely to know how to obtain birth control or even to know the basic facts related to sexual intercourse and its consequences (Farley 1987:214–15), and (2) the cost of birth control.

While teenage females who take courses in sex education tend to have a lower rate of sexual intercourse, working-class teenagers are still less likely to use contraceptives. In developing nations the best predictor of the female use of birth control is social class (Commoner 1974, Murdoch 1981, Quadeer 1975, Tierney 1986). That is, the best way of reducing birth rates is to improve people's economic opportunities and positions; education by itself has little effect.

23. As Petchesky writes, "The 'right-to-life' movement was originally a creation of the Family Life Division of the National Conference of Catholic Bishops (NCCB), the directing body of the Catholic Church in America" (1984:252). Petchesky goes on to point out that Catholic churches "constitute the most important strategic base for carrying out the antiabortion crusade" (253). As she states, churches provide (1) financial support, (2) an organizational and communication network, (3) infrastructural support, such as space, telephones, and other resources. Even more important is the symbolic power of religious organizations, their manipulation of cultural symbols (Etzioni 1968). The ability to promote and manipulate cultural symbols is one of the most basic sources of power, particularly in social movements.

24. According to Petchesky (1984:279n27), "Evidence in *McRae* [a suit aimed at revoking the tax-free status of the National Bishops Council] revealed an agreement between the New York Right to Life Committee and Cardinal Cooke that funds collected in churches on 'Respect for Life Sunday' would be split three ways between 'the local group,' the state committee, and the National Right-to-Life Committee" (*McRae* Brief, pp. 101–3).

25. As of May 1992, 12 states provided assistance to eligible women for abortions: Alaska, California, Connecticut, Hawaii, Massachusetts, New Jersey, New York, North Carolina, Oregon, Vermont, Washington, and West Virginia. Eight additional states provided assistance only for victims of rape

and those whose lives are threatened by the pregnancy. For an interview with Henry Hyde, see *60 Minutes,* 4 October 1981.

26. I have found very little research on the characteristics of anti-abortion activists, especially in the early stages of the movement following *Roe* and *Doe*. Most such research looks at those who are active at a particular time and in a very particular, often local, segment of the movement, usually a number of years into the movement, and does not distinguish between early and later activists or between those attracted to different movement segments/organization types. Luker (1984) examines the California activists, and many of my conclusions are generalizations from her findings in California. Thus, the reader should realize that these generalizations about the nation as a whole may not be completely valid. There is a need for research to determine if there are differences in those drawn to the movement at different periods of time and to different organizations with differing levels of activism and approaches to the issue. I will later suggest some likely hypotheses on this.

27. Anecdotal support for this theory is evidenced in my experience at the 1985 trial of several activists charged with bombing an abortion clinic in Pensacola, Florida. Of the more than 20 anti-abortion activists with whom I interacted there, all seemed to assume that I agreed with them. No one asked my opinion on the abortion issue, and several reacted with a sense of betrayal when they learned that I was pro-choice. In my interviews with arsonists and bombers the same pattern held; only one asked my position on abortion, and he interrupted me before I could complete one sentence. (See Blanchard and Prewitt 1993.)

28. In its 1989 *Webster* ruling, the Supreme Court upheld the Reagan administrative dictate that any facility receiving federal funds could not mention abortion as an option. The Court's ruling appears on its face to violate the essential basis of both *Roe* and *Doe,* the right to privacy. As Garfield and Hennessey (1984:9) assert: "the right to privacy is actually two rights: the individual's right not to have certain matters disclosed to the public or government, and the right to independence in making important and personal decisions, such as those pertaining to marriage and procreation."

29. John Danforth, then attorney general of Missouri, later became the Republican U.S. Senator who sponsored Clarence Thomas's nomination to the Supreme Court.

30. This requirement would presumably be unconstitutional in those six to nine states with explicitly defined privacy rights in their constitutions (see note 17 of in this chapter).

31. Faux (1988:332–33) cites the dissent of justices Brennan, Marshall, and Blackmun, which contends that the ruling on Maher constitutes denial of rights to those in poverty.

32. One facet of the current sociopolitical scene is that of "coming out of the closet." Women, including entertainment stars, who had abortions

when they were illegal are going public with their experiences; homosexuals are increasingly declaring themselves as such rather than keeping their sexual orientation to themselves. This means that persons who have had de facto rights are now demanding de jure rights. It appears that cultural fundamentalists are more concerned about and antagonistic toward the de jure (legal) status of certain issues than their de facto (practical but not legal) status.

Chapter 4

1. To my knowledge, there have been no studies of social distance among the organizations of any social movement.

2. Cable *et al.* (1988:951) point to at least two sources of recruitment: "utilitarian alliances grounded on shared grievances" and "existing friendship networks." These may vary in importance with level of involvement in the movement. Even "utilitarian alliances," however, which could be identical to Luker's category of "self-selection," may have their origins in pre-existing networks. Luker does not push her informants' information back to such possible sources.

3. Ginsburg (1990), for example, finds differential experiences of American society by different age cohorts to be a crucial factor in activists joining one organization or another. Among males involved in the anti-abortion movement, social class appears to be a crucial factor. Professionals, as mentioned earlier, are more likely to be involved in the educational and political action arms of the movement, while working-class males appear to dominate the more strident activists and those prone to violence. The type of occupation is also apparently crucial; that is, the more discretion a person has over his or her time, the more likely it is that he or she can be recruited into activism. Current research indicates that the more extreme the activism, the more discretionary time the activist is likely to have and the less threatened he or she is by a jail sentence (see Blanchard and Prewitt 1993). See also Seaton (1991) for a sociopsychological perspective on those who blockaded Vancouver, Canada, clinics. Maxwell (1991) finds that personal need is also a crucial factor in movement involvement. For example, some people may have a "need" to stand out or in some way become a public figure. Leahy (1975) finds that social networks are an important element in recruitment into the movement, especially for leaders.

4. The development of the anti-abortion movement has some parallels with the development of the civil rights movement of the 1950s, 1960s, and 1970s. The NAACP, composed primarily of African-Americans, initially included a significant number of whites, who may presumably be characterized as altruistic since they had little to gain personally from the empowerment of African-Americans. (A similar characterization could be made of associated organizations, such as the Urban League, the Fellowship of

Reconciliation, the Fellowship of Southern Churchmen, and the Christian Socialists.)

In the 1960s and 1970s the movement became increasingly activist and increasingly dominated by African-Americans, to the extent that whites were invited out of some organizations, such as the Student Nonviolent Coordinating Committee. (Whites were never much of a force in the Southern Christian Leadership Conference. For example, only one white, Will D. Campbell, executive director of the Committee of Southern Churchmen, was present at its organization.) That is, the movement became increasingly an expression of self-interest rather than altruism.

This is not to say that self-interest on the part of the disinherited or other minorities bears a negative connotation. Activists of any stripe, altruistic or self-interested, tend to be a minority who are frequently willing to take great risks, whether it be for themselves, for their social group, on behalf of others, or any combination of these. The vast majority of those who benefit from any social movement tend to be free-riders. On the other hand, one may make a qualitative judgment that the degree of honesty about one's self-interest in social movement involvement does have some ethical import.

The anti-abortion movement appears to have followed a similar pattern. It also began with predominantly middle-class organizations and gradually grew to include numerous organizations that were increasingly working-class based and increasingly activist and radical. Furthermore, the persons involved were less obviously altruistic in their motivations, moving from the original groups acting out of theological or philosophical commitments to ones primarily defending a life-style embedded in traditional cultural values. While movements may frequently arise out of shared interests and identities embedded in social networks, movements also clarify, focus, and elaborate those identities.(See, for example, Morris and Mueller 1992.) That is, the movement itself may give people an identity, a not unimportant social value.

5. In addition to the civil rights category Cuneo named a family heritage category (concerned with family and the status of women) and Catholic revivalists category. Revivalists are equivalent to Catholic fundamentalists, seeking to revitalize the Catholic church in Canada. Cuneo claims that the term *fundamentalist* is inappropriate to this group because it invites comparison with Protestant and Islamic fundamentalists. I maintain that the term is appropriate because, as Cuneo himself states, the Catholic revivalists share significant and key beliefs with Protestant fundamentalists; namely, "an inerrant Bible, the literal existence of a heaven and hell, and a demonic force active in the world personified as 'the devil'" (100). Cuneo also says that these Catholics have a "missionary zeal and ideology of crisis" (186). He adds that "the Revivalist imagination interprets everything in terms of a dualistic drama of light versus darkness. And in spiritual warfare, where everyone is aligned on the side of either angels or demons, there is

no point in sparing feelings or reputations, in passing over scandal, or in deferring to qualms of civility. The enemy must be exposed and brought to judgment" (191). The parallels are too striking to ignore and they do invite comparisons, as well as equalization, with Protestant and Islamic fundamentalists. As will be explained shortly, fundamentalism is characterized by just this kind of dualism.

6. The text under the heading "Religious and Cultural Fundamentalism Defined" is adapted from Blanchard and Prewitt (1993).

7. Many authors describe the basic elements of "documentary theory." See, for example, documentary treatment of Genesis, the first book of the Torah, in Gunkel (1910), von Rad (1972), and Coats (1983).

8. One of the most prominent founding documents of the Social Gospel is Rauschenbusch (1918).

9. The series was published between 1910 and 1915 (Dixon, Meyer, and Torrey). In 1895 a conference was held at Niagara, New York, which essentially outlined the basic tenets of fundamentalism and formed the basis of the series. See Cole (1963) and Gaspar (1963).

10. Ammerman (1991, 217) maintains that theology alone is an insufficient definition of fundamentalism, that it is significantly marked by organizing to oppose social change. Blanchard and Prewitt (1993) differ with this, contending that fundamentalism is essentially a theological and ideological stance, that mobilization and organization for activism among fundamentalists, as in other ideological orientations, depends on sociocultural and sociopsychological variables among the adherents.

11. Many also oppose the use of birth control, as will be discussed later in the chapter. Recent studies of church growth among the conservative denominations have concluded that their increasing membership, as opposed to the declining membership in more "mainline" churches, is based primarily on higher birth rates and the ability to hold onto young people past adolescence (Kelly 1977).

12. Studies have shown that both Protestant and Catholic abortion protesters value "traditional sexual morality"; that is, they oppose premarital sex, birth control for teenagers, sex education in the schools, and divorce (Granberg 1988, Fiedler and Pomerleau 1978).

Stets (1991) finds that they have a unitary, absolutist attitude structure and are more likely:

(1) to engage in black-white, categorical thinking, (2) to minimize attitude conflict (dissonant stimuli either fit a class or are excluded, thus there is relatively little ambiguity), (3) to anchor behavior in external conditions (thus restricting internal integrative processes and the self as causative agent in interpreting stimuli), and (4) to consider change as sometimes necessary. . . . Such individuals are interpreting the different issues in the same way; they see them as representing the same underlying dimension.

This underlying dimension might symbolize "adhering to authority," "following one's conscience," or "abiding by one's religious beliefs." . . . Pro-lifers may see that there is only one issue: doing the right thing as defined by those in authority.

13. Cuneo (1989) maintains that there are significant numbers of Catholics who share with Protestant fundamentalists a belief in and emphasis on biblical inerrancy, the physical resurrection of Jesus, and the requirement of a personal relationship with Jesus for salvation (42).

14. There is debate at present about the applicability of the term *fundamentalism* to religions, Christian and non-Christian, other than Protestantism. A number of scholars believe the term *fundamentalism* should be reserved for Protestants and exclude Catholics and non-Christians. Cuneo (1989) limits the term to Protestants. Others would disagree with that position.

Marty and Appleby (1992) maintain that while the term is applicable to some Jewish and Islamic groups, it should not include Protestant charismatics. I find it difficult to understand this exclusion, since they admit that charismatics generally share the major tenets of fundamentalism. Marty and Appleby maintain that the charismatics' openness to new revelations through the Holy Spirit set them apart. Nonetheless, all fundamentalists keep getting new insights from their sources of authority. Furthermore, charismatic groups are not all that free-wheeling. They are usually quite careful in controlling and regulating the revelations that are allowed to become "legitimate."

For example, the former pastor of First Assembly of God in Pensacola told me that he would not allow speaking in tongues to interrupt the sermon or prayers, for "The Spirit is orderly." That church also had a Sunday School class for training people in how to speak in tongues, which suggests something quite less than complete openness to just any "movement of the Spirit."

15. See, for example, Hunsberger and Altemeyer (1991). Lifton (1986) points out in his discussion of totalitarianism what is an interesting potential corollary with authoritarianism. Those who seek total control over others may well be frightened by their own dark, potentially uncontrollable urges. In fear of their own internal selves, they seek total control over their external world, especially other people. The fear of oneself may lead to a desire to institute one's omnipotence.

Indeed, there is an intimate relationship between authoritarianism and totalitarianism. The original studies of the authoritarian personality by Theodor W. Adorno *et al.* (1952) arose from interest in the behavior of the German people under the Nazis. Fundamentalism stresses obedience and submission to authority, usually in the form of a charismatic leader, not unlike German submission to Hitler.

Another tie between fundamentalism and totalitarianism is indicated by Lifton, who asserts that nazism was a form of "reactionary modernism" (494). That is, the Nazis used modern technology to its fullest in killing millions of people in an attempt to return to a "primitive" German myth. At heart, Lifton asserts, they were anti-technology and anti-modernism.

As Stets (1991:16) asserts, "Pro-lifers may see that there is only one issue: doing the right thing as defined by those in authority." She concludes that while it may be important to examine social movements from the resource mobilization perspective, "it is equally important to examine the individual actors in a movement and the extent to which their attitude structure influences a movement's activities."

16. As I have cited previously (Blanchard and Prewitt 1993), Marty (1987: 300) describes fundamentalism as "an almost Manichean world of black/white, God/Satan, Christ/Antichrist, Christian/'secular humanist.'"

I am surprised at how infrequently works on fundamentalism (e.g., Sandeen 1970, Jorstad 1970, and Caplan 1987) mention its Manichaean dualism. An exception is Fackre (1972). Manichaean or Zoroastrian dualism is commonly found in Jewish, Islamic, Sikh, and Hindu fundamentalisms, as well as in its Christian expressions.

Dualism in Christianity probably originates with the imposition of Greek, particularly Platonic, thought on the New Testament, as well as the influence of Zoroastrian thought on Judaism in the intratestamentary period (between the writing of the Old and the New Testament (c. 300 B.C.–A.D. 70). The Old Testament is clearly this-worldly and unitary in its view of human existence.

17. Dualism sees the world and its people caught in a cosmic war between good and evil, body and spirit, faith and reason. These dualisms originate in the merger of Greek and Christian thought in early Christianity and were exacerbated by Thomist theology. The "real" worlds in this pattern of thought are the ideal worlds of good, God, ideas, and spirituality rather than the observable physical world. Fundamentalism also tends to personalize these forces. Thus, many fundamentalists assume the existence of angels and demons.

18. I do not mean to claim that all or even most fundamentalists are prone to or support violence. I only maintain that the thought pattern encourages violence in the suggestible and in those already prone to violence, especially those who are socially isolated.

19. A number of biblical scholars actually deny the existence of an eternal hell in either the Old or New Testaments.

20. In fundamentalist theology sins are defined as crimes against society. Therefore, the tendency in recent decades to decriminalize "victimless" crimes, such as cohabitation and homosexuality, are viewed with alarm by fundamentalists. At the same time, they find their own moral codes being mitigated. For example, fundamentalists will be found shopping in department stores on Sunday after church, and women in denominations that once eschewed makeup, such as the Assemblies of God, now have them attending church in such. Tammy Bakker is probably the extreme example of this change.

21. There are interesting parallels between schools of sociological theory and various theologies. For example, there is an inherent pessimism about human nature in structural functionalism in its assumption that social structure is needed to control and limit human selfishness and greed. Thus, order is necessary to keep people from doing wrong. Fundamentalism also has a preoccupation with control. It wants to limit sexual expression, for example; otherwise the natural human bent toward sin will rise to the fore. Ignorance of sexuality is thought to prevent promiscuity, and fear of the punishment of public disdain for premarital pregnancy is thought to keep women chaste. Both structural functionalism and cultural fundamentalism also emphasize the importance of social stability and a natural resistance to change.

On the other hand, conflict theory assumes that human nature is basically good and that the real problem is "bad" social structures. Witness Karl Marx's vision of the classless society of the future when every individual person would contribute his or her best for the social good and would demand from society only what he or she needs. This society would have no need of religion or the state to keep people in line. This is somewhat comparable with liberal theology's goal of the availability of the widest choice for individual self-fulfillment and a reduction in the laws prohibiting "victimless" crimes, such as homosexuality. In these views, change is essential and a basic, positive reality of social life.

Both positions are rather extreme and idealistic. More realistic in social theory is the systems model, which asserts that there is a degree of truth in both of the above, but that both change and stability are necessary to social life and social order.

22. Social Darwinism, the origins of which predate Charles Darwin, opposes assistance to the poor and other "less fortunates" on various grounds, including the classic religious proposition that people are in poverty because they have sinned and are being punished by God, and the more overtly racist and secular proposition that it is better for the weak to die out to prevent them from degrading the human species with their progeny, a misuse of Darwin's proposition of natural selection. Some have characterized those observing this position as opposing abortion, Aid to Dependent Children, prenatal health care, and other social welfare programs.

23. Redekop (1968) points to three basic ties between fundamentalism and the radical right: (1) a simplistic dualism that sees virtually everything in a stark, black-white dichotomy, (2) a conspiratorial view of the world, and (3) individualism. The notion of individualism needs some qualification. For while both groups emphasize the rights of individuals to operate in the economic sphere without governmental regulation and the importance of the individual's spiritual experience, the extremists of both groups would impose their definitions of morality in a collective fashion—thereby negating the rights of the individual.

24. When one Operation Rescue member was asked if he would approve of abortion for a "12-year-old rape victim whose health would be harmed by a full-term pregnancy," he responded: "I hope you don't think we're being insensitive. . . . We're aware of what the flip side is. It comes back to the matter of absolutes. It's just easier to have a blanket absolute, which Scripture provides, than to grapple with these tough questions" (Morris 1989).

Falik (1975) found that anti-abortionists were characterized by "conventionalism, authoritarian submission, exaggerated identification with masculine and feminine stereotypes, extreme emphasis on discipline, and a moralistic rejection of the impulse life" ("impulse life" refers to self-assertion, lack of obedience to authority); they also demonstrated a "degree of religious identification" and "an inability to tolerate ambiguity."

Johnson and Tamney (1984, 1988:44) found that those with "inconsistent life views," such as opposing abortion while favoring the death penalty, "tend to be authoritarian, and dogmatic authoritarians tend to ignore or compartmentalize inconsistent beliefs."

25. Frenkel-Brunswick (1954) found that authoritarian children, who usually come from authoritarian families, "tend to display authoritarian aggression, rigidity, cruelty, superstition, externalization and projectivity, denial of weakness, power orientation and more often hold dichotomous conceptions of sex roles, of kinds of people, and of values" (237). Lifton and Strozier (1990) conclude from their work at the Center on Violence and Human Survival that fundamentalism comes "close to sadism" (25). They also find that fundamentalism has "the need for total control of children."

26. A similar philosophy is espoused by John Burt's Our Father's House. One of his brochures asserts, "They [the Burts] set down and enforce house rules that help the individual develop self-discipline" ("Welcome to Our Father's House," n.d.). Residents are not allowed to send or receive mail or telephone calls without Burt's censoring; may not leave the house unaccompanied or without permission; may not have another person, even of the same sex, in their room with the door closed, and may not touch the house television channel setting (set on a Christian network). In addition, they must turn over all income, such as welfare payments, to the house. In short, they assume that total dependence is the pathway for the development of responsible independence.

27. Sociologist Everett Hughes once said, "Every child has an inalienable right to authoritarian parents against whom to rebel."

28. See de Berg (1990) for the importance of the position of women in the origins of fundamentalism. De Berg argues, based on early documents of the fundamentalist movement, that early twentieth-century fundamentalism was primarily a reaction to the changing roles of women, as opposed to the usual assumption that it was a reaction to the larger issue of modernism. Of course, it can easily be argued that the change in the roles of women was just

one of the many results of the complex of changes wrought by modernism. While many of the early fundamentalists may have focused on female roles as the central problem (possibly because it was the most obvious and personally threatening), others quickly saw that the issue was larger and deeper.

29. There are disagreements in the research on this issue. They may arise over the subjects of the different investigations. It is likely, for example, that upper-middle-class Catholics, who are more apt to be involved in the educational and political efforts of the movement, function out of a broad "pro-life" ideology and motivation, while the more activist, working-class Catholics, who are more likely to picket or participate in more violent activities, operate out of an ethic centering on sexual behavior and the status of women. As Ellen Willis noted in the *Village Voice*, "the nitty-gritty issue in the abortion debate is not life but sex" (cited in Petchesky 1984:263). Her observation may apply primarily to the more activist wing of the movement. Johnson and Tamney (1988) hypothesize that those with "inconsistent" life views "are not really as concerned with the life-taking aspect of abortion as with their opinion that abortion promotes sexual promiscuity. These people are not so much 'right-to-lifers' as sexual moralizers" (44–45).

30. Johnson and Tamney (1988:44–45) write that those with inconsistent life views (opposing abortion while affirming the death penalty, for instance) share four traits: (1) membership in fundamentalist Protestant churches, (2) concern about the sexual behavior of young adults, (3) belief in physical force to solve problems, and (4) social traditionalism.

31. Hall and Ferree (1986:201) hold that "attitude toward premarital sexual relations becomes the best predictor of abortion attitudes for both blacks and whites."

32. Lawrence (1989:100) maintains that one of five basic traits common to all religious fundamentalists is "secondary-level male elites. They derive authority from a direct, unmediated appeal to scripture, yet because interpretive principles are often vague, they must be clarified by charismatic leaders who are invariably male." The ideology of male dominance extends well beyond the masculine elite; an exaggerated masculinity infuses the entire ideology itself.

The official pronouncements of both the Catholic and Mormon churches support male dominance in the family. The literature of the various religious segments of the anti-abortion movement, as well as the public utterances of its leaders, lend overwhelming support to this point.

33. Fear is an important component of the entire fundamentalist syndrome—fear of Satan's wiles, fear of pregnancy outside marriage, fear of the wrath of God, fear of the consequences of any form of disobedience. Barbara Ehrenreich (1983) says that the easy availability of abortion "has upset a system in which the only 'honorable' outcome of an unwanted pregnancy is marriage" (cited in Joffe 1985).

34. Cuneo (1989) maintains that the "family heritage" Catholics involved in the Toronto anti-abortion movement are those primarily interested in maintaining the "traditional" family status of males and females. The females, in particular, desire to hold both males and females responsible for their sexual behavior in defense of their prized mothering roles.

Komarovsky (1964) describes vividly the blue-collar women who place priority on their mothering role. They view their husbands in a utilitarian fashion, prizing and evaluating them primarily on their ability to provide the means for the women to perform their mothering role.

35. An interesting development likely affecting the dynamic of male dominance in the home is that of the majority of married women, especially in the working class, working outside the home. Research has verified that power in the family tends to shift from the husband to the wife with the proportion of family income brought home by the woman. This dissonance could lead to those males caught in such a circumstance trying even harder to assert their weakening authority. If they cannot do so at home, they may seek to do so in the wider anti-abortion movement.

36. The Catholic church has since 1867 opposed the use of contraceptives. The Catholic position is derived from the church's concept of "natural law," which holds that some moral principles can be deduced from the observation of "nature" and do not require a direct revelation from God to be declared "right" or "wrong." Insofar as the Catholic church's stance on sexuality, the reasoning goes that (1) animals naturally copulate to procreate (while it is obvious that animals have no knowledge of the connection between copulation and conception, natural theology would hold that any pleasure they derive from the experience was divinely intended to secure procreation and that human pleasure in copulation serves the same role); (2) humans are animals and experience pleasure in their sexuality; therefore, (3) human pleasure in sexuality is divinely intended as an instrument toward the end of conception; and, therefore, (4) anything that unnaturally or artificially interferes with conception is contrary to nature and the will of God. This concept of natural theology arose as a basic supposition of Catholic theology during medieval times in the thought of Thomas Aquinas and has remained a major force since then. It should be noted, however, that the majority of American Catholics ignore the church's pronouncements on birth control and abortion; Catholic women resort to both with the same frequency as Protestant women (Catholics for a Free Choice 1986:9, 12).

Protestants and Jews have generally accepted the use of birth control. Fundamentalist Protestants and Mormons generally qualify the use of birth control. They share a valuation of the traditional family in which the mother concentrates on that role by not working outside the home. This also involves large families. Thus, while fundamentalist Protestants and Mormons may occasionally use birth control for child spacing, there is a general ethos against its use. (The fundamentalist attitude toward birth control differs markedly from that of the broader group of nonfundamentalist evangelicals, who generally accept the use of birth control.)

Neitz's explanation for the anti-abortion movement's opposition to abortion also applies to the opposition of some to birth control: "[It] breaks the connection between sex and procreation, denies the sanctity of motherhood and the authority of the father, and implies that it is the individual and not the family which is the basic social unit" (1981:265).

37. A CNN report on 14 December 1991 stated that there had been a drastic drop in the rate of female births in India as a result of fetal sex determination and the abortion of female fetuses. See also "Fetal Scan," 28 April 1991.

38. Violence against abortion clinics and physicians' offices in Pensacola, Florida, for example, was preceded by almost 10 years of arsons of gay bars. (See Blanchard and Prewitt 1993, Bruce 1988, Clarke 1987, Conway 1982, Diamond 1989, Fields 1991, Granberg 1978, Jaffe *et al.* 1981, Jorstad 1970, LaHaye 1980, Lawrence 1989, Liebman 1983, Neitz 1981, Smidt 1989, Spitzer 1987, van Til 1967a, 1967b, 1967c.)

39. See the segment "On Earth as It Is in Heaven" from Bill Moyers's *God and Politics* series on PBS (1988). In this program he interviews a number of Christian Reconstructionists, including Rousas John Rushdoony, considered the father of reconstructionism, and illuminates some of the disagreements among them. The prominent theologian of the movement is Cornelius van Til. The discussion of Christian Reconstructionism in the text is from Blanchard and Prewitt (1993).

40. The influence of their major authors, especially Rushdoony, extends to the larger fundamentalist community.

41. Rushdoony disagrees with Gary North on this point and would not impose reconstructionism anti-democratically. Rushdoony has written more than 30 books. Other prominent authors and figures in the movement include North, David Chilton, and Robert Thoburn.

42. Rushdoony unabashedly asserts that democracy is "the great love of the failures and cowards of life" and that Christianity is basically and radically anti-democratic. "It is committed to a spiritual aristocracy" (Moyers 1988). Fields (1991) supports the contention that fundamentalists seek to reinstitute the dominance of religion over all other social institutions.

Chapter 5

1. It is worth noting here that even educated professionals in an urban, multicultural society may exist in relative isolation from those influences. See the discussion of encapsulation in chapter 7.

2. The National Abortion Federation, founded by abortion providers as

a source of mutual national support, keeps statistical records on the varieties of anti-abortion-related violence and regularly surveys clinics across the nation and the Bureau of Alcohol, Tobacco and Firearms for this information. While the statistics may be somewhat skewed by the self-interests of reporting clinics, the trends they reveal are probably fairly accurate.

3. For one activist's justification for bombings, see CNN's *Crossfire* program of 4 January 1985. For other, broader justifications, see Blanchard and Prewitt (1993).

4. Muller and Godwin (1984:140–41) maintain that "persons who are alienated from the political system, who perceive themselves to have insufficient political power, and whose ideology accepts political violence, should be predisposed to participate in aggressive political behavior. This would be especially true where they perceive such behavior as effective methods for achieving political goals and when they have available time to pursue these activities. Conversely, persons who believe that their participation in governmental decision making is important, who perceive that they have influence on those decisions, and who are not only interested in politics but supportive of the political system, belong to relevant organizations, and have attained the education necessary for acceptance by other participants, are likely to exhibit above average levels of democratic participation."

5. These conclusions are offered as educated guesses or hypotheses, for to my knowledge there has been no comprehensive research on the movement as a whole.

Chapter 6

1. According to English (1981:20) the National Committee for the Human Life Amendment, an arm of the NRLC, itself received $277,000 from Catholic dioceses.

2. Operation Rescue received $10,000 from Jerry Falwell to help pay its fines and legal expenses for arrests in Atlanta in 1988 (Thomas 1988).

3. Law enforcement officials usually react to these conferences with deep resentment, because of the appearance that Operation Rescue is "in charge" and making the police a part of its script. One of the most effective tactics against Operation Rescue, used in Baton Rouge and Wichita, was the placing of a high chain-link fence around the targeted clinics, which prevented demonstrators from reaching the clinic doors. This tactic depended on supporting court orders.

4. RICO was enacted by Congress primarily to attack organized crime and its "front" organizations in attempts to criminally take over legitimate businesses, but federal courts have upheld broader applications of the law. On 10 October 1989, the Supreme Court upheld the use of RICO laws against 26 defendants in incidents at a Philadelphia clinic *(Pensacola News*

Journal, 11 October 1989:2A). The basis of the suit was conspiracy to shut down a legal business.

5. Fines in New York City alone were $500,000 (*National NOW Times,* March/April 1991:2). Adele Nathanson, wife of Bernard Nathanson (formerly a primary provider of abortions in New York City and now an anti-abortionist), was fined and paid $25,000 in the same case.

6. For descriptions of what happens in a number of such "clinics," see *Primetime Live,* "Lying in Wait," 31 October 1991 and Abas (1985).

7. A Human Life International ad blames the shortage of priests in the Catholic church on abortion ("Notebook" 1990).

8. Ryan later left his wife and a six-week-old infant to marry the woman, who was already divorcing her husband.

9. Personal conversation with sociologist Carol Maxwell, 12 November 1992.

10. See *60 Minutes,* 14 August 1977. When questioned about the "fairness" of this denial of federal aid to poor women, Carter responded, "Life isn't fair."

11. The announcement of the effectiveness of RU-486 resulted in increased publicity for Ovral, a high-hormone pill, as a "morning after" abortifacient. The patient takes two Ovral pills within 72 hours and two more 12 hours later. Ovral has potential side effects of nausea, vomiting, and headache (*Pensacola News Journal,* 12 October 1992).

12. I should note, however, that the Bureau of Alcohol, Tobacco, and Firearms did an excellent job of solving a number of the violent incidents and that that agency and the FBI maintained a joint task force and office on developing a profile of those anti-abortion activists likely to commit violence (Blanchard and Prewitt 1993).

13. Vermont and New Jersey governors announced plans to increase state funding for Planned Parenthood offices to offset federal reductions (Planned Parenthood 1992a), and the Arizona Senate approved similar funding (Planned Parenthood 1991).

14. Shupe and Heinerman (1985) maintain that the Moral Majority and Mormons were connected through the John Birch Society. See Snowball (1991:31–60) for a review of the conflicting accounts of the origins of the Moral Majority. See also Diamond (1989).

15. Snow and Benford (1992) indicate the importance of the "master frame" of a social movement. The master frame, they assert, is "an interpretive schemata that simplifies and condenses the 'world out there'" (137). Such frames, then, are maps through which events are interpreted. They are similar to what Boulding (1964) means by an ideology, a drama that includes a script and roles for participants to play in the drama. As such, frames also limit the potential actions of movement members. By left-handedly endorsing the arsonists and bombers of clinics, the leaders of the less violent organizations

in the movement in effect enlarged the acceptable behavior of the anti-abortion frame to include violent actions. Thus, the frame allows virtually any action, and in this context the clinic blockades and picketing of groups such as Operation Rescue are perceived as being milder and therefore more acceptable. Such an open master frame allows for virtually unlimited innovation in tactics and strategies, which in turn indicates longevity for the movement.

16. National denominational pronouncements on race relations had little effect, if any, on individual beliefs and attitudes in the southern sectors of those denominations. This is easily explained by the consensus held at the local congregational level. The abortion issue, however, is not sectional, even though there is greater support for the anti-abortion stance in the South than elsewhere. Within practically every congregation, especially of the mainline denominations, people are likely to openly and nonvituperatively disagree on the issue. One indicant of the lack of the power of official pronouncements to sway people lies in the fact that Catholics differ relatively little from Protestants in their abortion attitudes and virtually none at all in the frequency with which they seek them.

17. It is important to note that those small groups involved in extreme violence, bombings and arsons, tended to be unidenominational. This is likely because of the need to remain inordinately secretive to avoid detection and arrest, requiring that the group be close-knit. It is also worth noting that the majority of such violence has been committed by Protestant fundamentalists and that violence increased after Protestant involvement in the movement (Blanchard and Prewitt 1993). It is also noteworthy that Catholic Evangelical/Protestant Fundamentalist coalitions formed through the anti-abortion movement promise to lead to cooperation on other common issues, particularly those related to family issues, while the traditional Catholic/Protestant coalition on issues such as peace, civil rights, and economics appears to be collapsing (Cimino 1991:3).

18. In 1992, Willke formed the Life Issues Institute to counter the "who decides" rhetoric of pro-choice groups (Planned Parenthood 1992d). The "who decides" campaign was designed to appeal to the American public's valuation of personal freedom and choice.

19. For example, in 1934 the Fellowship of Reconciliation, a strictly nonviolent organization, expelled Rheinhold Niebuhr and Howard Kester, their southern field representative, because they were willing to accept violence in self-defense in a Tennessee coal-mining strike in which deputies murdered the union leader on a public street. Niebuhr responded by organizing his own committee to raise support for Kester.

20. For example, studies of small groups have shown that there is an optimum functional size of 20–30. If such groups do not divide, then as new members join, they will either stay a short time and depart or old members will begin to drop out, keeping the membership size fairly stable. If groups

that have reached maximum size split, however, each of the new groups will tend to grow to the 20–30 size. While this clearly does not apply to groups such as the NRLC, with a large, widely dispersed coterie of members that do not interact on a regular, intimate basis, the processes are similar with groups that have limited goals and focuses; this effectively shuts out persons who may subscribe to the ultimate goals of a group but who would support different tactics and strategies.

21. This is a clear example of blaming the victim, just as some blame the rape victim because for being "wrong"—in the wrong place, at the wrong time, or in the wrong clothes.

22. Burt stated to me in 1985 that he would bomb a clinic if he thought he could get away with it. Randall Terry said in a California speech, "We may have passed the window where America can be restored without bloodshed . . . I don't know whose blood may need to be shed" (Corbin 1993:5). In 1985 (Frame 1985:45) Cal Thomas compared clinic bombings with "the riots of blacks during civil rights protests but served a higher and nobler purpose in that they moved lethargic government leaders to action. . . . The fact is that if [abortionists] hadn't slaughtered 15 million babies, there wouldn't be any buildings being blown up." Jan Carroll of the NRLC added, "The violence which goes on inside the clinic is much more damaging to the moral fiber of this nation."

Jayne Bray, an officer of Operation Rescue in 1989, is the wife of Michael Bray, who served a prison term for bombing clinics in the Washington, D.C., area. They named one of their children Beseda Bray after Curtis Beseda, another early clinic bomber, and Bray told me that his wife had visited Curtis Beseda in prison several times.

23.Any effective movement organization is conscious of playing to a wide variety of audiences and seeks to garner support from as many as possible. Thus, rhetoric and use of the media are important.

Chapter 7

1. Blanchard and Prewitt (1993) maintain that

As Joseph Fichter (1954) reported in his study of Catholic parishes, organizations have multileveled constituencies. At the outer edge of a parish, for example, are those non-Catholics for whom the parish bears some responsibility, such as spouses or children of Catholics. As one moves through concentric circles from the outer ring toward the center, the degree of involvement and commitment to the church increases. In the inner circle are the most committed, fully practicing members.

Social movements also have multilayered constituencies and participants. At the outer edge are those who support its goals but are not actively involved in movement organizations. They may support the movement in voting or other political behavior, but they do not consider it a primary motivating factor. As you move toward the core of the movement, behavior grows more activist and more radical. Organizations established to support the movement have different levels of commitment to its objectives, will use different tactics to achieve the goals, and will, therefore, be found spread out through the various inner-to-outer circles.

However, all the other movement organizations and supporters will find themselves having to react to the behavior of movement supporters and organizations more extremist than they are. And "moderate" organizations may find it necessary to become more radical to maintain their own constituencies. The more moderate organizations may find themselves superseded in the public eye, and even their own reputations characterized, by more extremist groups. Individuals may move inward from one level of activism to a more activist behavior. On the other hand, other persons may not involve themselves at all in the outer organizations, but may leap into a super-activist position. Newcomers to a movement may feel a compulsion to jump beyond current levels of activism to prove their identification with the movement (what sociologists call the conversion syndrome).

At different stages of social movement development, different persons with different levels of commitment and activism, as well as different social profiles, will be attracted to organizations related to it. Willingness to become active in a movement will depend, at least partially, on one's social position and relations within the society and the relative costs of becoming active. Earlier "activists" may withdraw as more persons willing to escalate the level or stage of activism become involved and are willing to escalate toward greater degrees of radicalism. Also, as more extreme behavior develops in the movement, persons who might have united with less radical organizations may well pull back from being mobilized because of the entire movement's being identified with the radicals. Thus, the early, more civil, activists may serve to recruit increasingly less civil members and move an organization beyond their own dreams and ambitions.

On the other hand, extremists, by attracting the primary attention of countervailing authorities, may serve to free up more moderate members and organizations to a higher degree of activism. That is, extreme behavior, as pointed out by Killian (1972), may allow a redefinition of the situation in which slightly less extreme behavior now appears more or less moderate in comparison when it would have previously been defined as most extreme (253–54).

2. Feminists for Life of America grew out of a number of anti-abortion National Organization for Women members who were expelled from NOW in 1972. They support both the equal rights amendment and the human life amendment.

3. The Bishops' Conference received a lot of negative reactions when it contracted with a public relations firm in 1991 for $5 million to help them determine how to attack the abortion issue.

4. At least some in the anti-abortion movement see the vigils as a recruitment device. Sharon Glass, a longtime anti-abortion activist and organizer in the Pensacola, Florida, area states: "Life Chain is a first step for people who want to get involved in the pro-life movement. They may be fearful of getting in a picket or a march or confronting people" (Goodwin 1992).

5. One interesting sidelight of the study of social movements is the rise of capitalistic entrepreneurial profit-making enterprises to service them. *Silent Scream*, for example, at first sold 3,000 copies at $400 each (Macdonald 1985). Other by-products of the movement include full-color postcards of bloody fetuses at 25 cents each, color picketing posters, and audio- and video-tapes available from a wide variety of organizations.

6. Operation Rescue spokespersons, and those of similar organizations and some bombers and arsonists, maintain that they are simply practicing freedom of speech and civil disobedience, as did the protesters of the civil rights movement. Civil disobedience, however, requires that the perpetrator (1) be completely nonviolent, (2) seek arrest for violation of the unjust law, and (3) have a fundamental respect for the law by seeking to suffer the consequences for the violation.

7. As Muller and Godwin (1984) assert: "persons who are alienated from the political system, who perceive themselves to have insufficient political power, and whose ideology accepts political violence, should be predisposed to participate in aggressive political behavior. This would be especially true where they perceive such behavior as effective methods for achieving political goals and when they have available time to pursue these activities. Conversely, persons who believe that their participation in governmental decision making is important, who perceive that they may have influence on those decisions, and who are not only interested in politics but supportive of the political system, belong to relevant organizations, and have attained the education necessary for acceptance by other participants, are likely to exhibit above average levels of democratic participation" (140–41).

8. Research on criminals indicates that professional criminals are the least rehabilitative because they lack permanent ties to families or to any specific community and thus find it difficult to be integrated into "normal" society. Encapsulation may be either voluntary or involuntary. For example, some religious fundamentalists intentionally limit their significant relationships to members of their own religious group. On the other hand, some radical students in the 1960s found themselves encapsulated by the negative reactions of family and friends to their protest activities (Goffman 1981).

9. As Kriesberg (1978) points out: "Antiabortion leaders are not isolates: they usually have families, most have lived in their neighborhoods at least five years, and they tend to join organizations in which they play leadership roles. Activists usually have an occupation that allows considerable time for movement work" (149). Such integration into relationships and organizations does not, however, prevent encapsulation. Indeed, all those encapsulated ties heighten the likelihood of their being recruited into activism.

10. Zald *et al.* have pointed out the distinction between a social movement organization (SMO) and a social movement industry (SMI). I hypothesize that there is an additional phenomenon that might be called a social

movement complex (SMC). An SMI, as the term has been used in the literature, is generally related to *single-issue* movements, such as the abolitionist, prohibition, and gun control movements and countermovements. An SMO refers to a single organization that is usually a part of an SMI.

Individual organizations, however, may span a number of issues and establish linkages with a number of SMIs. Thus, we may speak of the feminist social movement complex, which concerns itself with a diverse set of issues, including pro-choice movement, pay equity, maternal leave, and women's health care. Similarly, there is a traditional family complex that unites around such issues as pornography, abortion, anti-feminism, sex education, prayer, and homosexuality. Pro-life would then be the complex of organizations that come together over the anti-abortion, anti-nuclear, and anti-death penalty issues.

Some groups may be on opposite sides on one issue and united on others, such as NOW and Feminists for Life on the abortion issue, or united on one issue and on opposite sides on others, such as the NRLC and the Moral Majority, which agree on abortion and disagree on the other "pro-life" issues.

Curtis and Zurcher (1973) point to the importance of multiorganizational fields; that is, potential linkages of an SMO with other community organizations. SMOs that recruit through organizational linkages are more successful than those that recruit through individual contacts. SMCs may increase potential multiorganization fields.

SMCs have a structural flexibility: as new issues under their umbrella arise, they may mobilize new, previously immobilized or quiescent constituencies, thus enlarging their sway and overall impact, especially by changing the external perception of their strength and support. Additionally, a victory in one area strengthens the possibility of victory in others by attracting new supporters and impressing power brokers. A potential danger, however, lies in trying to mobilize on too many issues too quickly, which may give the impression of collective paranoia. Furthermore, loss in one area may diminish authority in all other areas. On the other hand, having multiple issues makes organizational survival more likely, though perhaps weakened, in defeat on any one issue. Indeed, defeat, if properly played out, can revitalize a movement. A case in point is the March of Dimes. The discovery of the polio vaccine was an organizational defeat, as it took away the organization's reason for being. The development of a new goal, effecting treatment for children with birth defects, which can never be completely "cured," led to organizational revitalization. The conditions under which defeat may be turned into mobilization need to be addressed more than they have.

SMOs depend at least partially for their existence on opposition SMOs. SMO development is an interactive process. Nothing unites people as quickly as a common enemy, making previously major differences and distinctions seem minor, stimulating the development of previously unlikely coalitions;

Catholics and Protestant fundamentalists on the abortion issue are a good example. Multiple-issue SMOs have the advantage of multiple enemies.

Questions remain unanswered: What type of SMO is most likely to have multiple issues? The professional SMO? Are professional SMOs, with a more sophisticated, full-time staff, more likely to perceive interrelationships among various issues and enlarge the areas of concern? How are coalitions formed among SMOs that agree on only one issue? Does such limited agreement lead to a tentative commitment to the SMI? A hesitancy to commit resources? Do single-issue SMOs commit a larger share of resources? Do single-issue SMOs form the power nucleus, leaving multiple-issue SMOs on the edge of the SMI?

11. For theoretical discussions of these issues, see Zald (1980) and Zald and Ash (1966).

12. The RICO charges were not added to the original suit until 1989 (Smith and McGraw 1989). The first RICO suit, to my knowledge, was filed by a Philadelphia clinic. In March 1989, the Third Circuit Court of Appeals upheld the liability of demonstrators there for fines and expenses of $108,000 under the RICO Act.

13. In October 1992 the Supreme Court heard oral arguments, for a second time, in this case. The Justice Department argued that the resolution of the matters in dispute should be left to the several state courts. The court determined that the issues were subject to federal rather than state laws and that the Ku Klux Klan laws did not apply in these cases.

14. For a more detailed analysis of the rhetoric of the anti-abortion and the pro-choice movements, see Granberg (1982), Granberg and Granberg (1981), Conditt (1990), Vanderford (1989), Lake (1986), Tumulty (1989), and Diamond (1989).

15. A federal court judge in Georgia ruled in October 1992 that the political television ads of Daniel Becker, a Republican candidate for the U.S. House of Representatives, which graphically depicted an abortion, could be shown only between midnight and 6 A.M. In the same month, within a few days of one another, a federal district judge ruled that the ad was indecent, and a circuit court of appeals referred the case to Supreme Court Justice Anthony Kennedy, who denied a hearing on the district court decision without any comment.

16. The relationships between a social movement and the media can be extremely complicated. See, for example, Gitlin (1980) and Ryan (1991).

17. In traditional sociological terms, relatively quiet picketing may be considered a *rite of maintenance,* while the escalated activism becomes a *rite of intensification,* similar to church services at Christmas and Easter and the relationship of July 4th celebrations to patriotism.

18. It is likely that most of the physicians who perform clinic abortions are "out-of-towners," because physicians who perform abortions within their own town are more subject to such sanctions.

19. As already stated, I contend that those groups most likely to support other groups are those which are closest to one another in their anti-abortion positions. These responses from Right to Life delegates indicate that they are closer to the violent wing than their official positions and their leadership are willing to admit.

Chapter 8

1. Of course, there are non-Catholics and nonfundamentalists active in the movement who would not share these positions.

2. One dramatic example of this was Father Coughlin, the Catholic priest who became famous for his anti-Semitic stances through his nation-wide broadcasts in the 1930s.

3. Mainline denominations dominated radio and early television through such programs as *The Protestant Hour* and Harry Emerson Fosdick's and Bishop Sheen's weekly shows. These programs, while popular in their heydays, were soon eclipsed by the greater drama and showmanship of the likes of Oral Roberts.

4. As Jenkins (1983) points out, "Movements must . . . walk the fine line between outlandishness (which alienates third parties but secures cover-age) and conventionality (which may be persuasive but is ignored by the media). . . . Media coverage also tends to make superstars out of leaders, aggravating internal rivalries and tendencies toward showmanship, thereby weakening mobilization."

5. It is likely that the authorities were aware of these operations, just as the police generally knew who was selling liquor during prohibition and have always known the identities of a community's prostitutes and bookies. So-called victimless crimes are usually tolerated, yet controlled.

6. This conclusion is supported by Leahy and Mazur (1978) and by Kriesberg (1978), who states that "anti-abortionists are apparently less con-cerned about abortion per se than with its legalization, which signifies, to them, a decline in traditional American religious and moral values, as well as governmental intrusion into private affairs—especially the family." According to Blanchard and Prewitt (1993),

There is something to be said for this approach to morality since it allows both sides of a dispute to develop a *modus vivendi*. For example, those on the inside of religious organizations—both lay and clerical—have known there were homosexual ministers. But it was no issue as long as they kept their homosexual activities outside the parish and outside the public purview; i.e., were "discreet." Now that homosexuals (even some homosexual ministers) are coming "out of the closet" and demanding public, as opposed to private, rights and statutory recognition, a great deal of strife and argumen-tation [has] arisen within religious and public groups. It is, at least in part, a dispute revolving around disagreements over *de facto* and *de jure* rights. Essentially, the same change is occurring regarding abortion. Indeed, one mark of deep social transformation in the current United States society may be the sheer number of issues for which organized groups are seeking as never before *de jure* rights: abortion, homosexuality, prostitution, pornography, and atheism, to name but a few. (150)

7. For discussions of the issue, see *Nightline,* 6 January 1988, and *Good Morning America,* 25 July 1991.

Chapter 9

1. In North Dakota, some women may travel 6 to 10 hours to reach a clinic (Salholz 1992). It is worth reiterating that abortion clinics are available in only 17 percent of the counties in the United States. This raises the question of what the Supreme Court considers an "undue burden."

2. In Pensacola, the NOW chapter has picketed the primary churches involved in the anti-abortion movement. In Orange County, California, an interfaith organization, the Coalition against Christian Violence, visits fundamentalist churches used by Operation Rescue for meetings and recruitment. Taking reporters with them, they distribute a letter to attendees indicating the church's support for Operation Rescue and asking for dialogue. After two or three consecutive visits, it is reported, the church usually withdraws from Operation Rescue activities (Courry 1991). In 1993 another California group blockaded the meeting site for an Operation Rescue planning meeting and forced the group to find another time and place to meet.

3. The murder of Dr. David Gunn in Pensacola in March 1993 and the wounding of Dr. George Tiller in Wichita in August 1993 appear to have had the following effects: more rapid consideration of the freedom of choice bill and of state laws that would assure clinic access, loss of some public support for the anti-abortion movement and its more radical tactics, distancing by less activist anti-abortion groups from support for groups approving violence, short-term invigoration of the pro-choice movement, and, possibly, an increase of violence by the more radical wing.

The attacks on Gunn and Tiller have motivated law enforcement officials to apply stalking laws to those following patients and clinic staff members. This could lead to a more active role for the FBI in clinic cases and a redefinition of clinic violence as terrorism.

References

Abas, Bryan. 1985. "Right to Life or Right to Lie?" *Progressive,* June, 24–25.

Adorno, Theodor W., *et al.* 1950. *The Authoritarian Personality.* New York: Harper.

Albert, M., D. Hanley, and M. Rothbart. 1986. "Gender Differences in Moral Reasoning." *Sex Roles* 15: 645–53.

Ammerman, Nancy Tatom. 1991. "Southern Baptists and the New Christian Right." *Review of Religious Research* 32, no. 3 (March): 213–36.

Barkan, Eileen. 1986. "Interorganizational Conflict in the Southern Civil Rights Movement." Sociological Inquiry 56: 190–209.

Barnes, Fred. 1987. "Bringing Up Baby." *New Republic,* 24 August, 10–12.

Bart, Pauline B. 1987. "Seizing the Means of Reproduction: An Illegal Feminist Abortion Collective—How and Why It Worked." *Qualitative Sociology* 10, no. 4 (Winter): 339–57.

Beal, C., A. Garrod, and Patrick Shin. 1990. "Development of Moral Orientation in Elementary School Children." *Sex Roles* 18: 13–27.

Bennetts, Leslie. 1981. "Antiabortion Forces in Disarray Less than a Year after Victories in Election." *New York Times,* 22 September.

Berger, Joseph. 1986. "Centers' Abortion Ads Called 'Bogus.'" *New York Times,* 16 July.

Bernstein, Carl. "The Holy Alliance." *Time,* February 1992, 28–35.

Blakely, Mary Kay. 1990. In "Hers," "Remembering Jane." *New York Times Magazine,* 23 September, 26, 78.

Blanchard, Dallas A., and Terry J. Prewitt. 1993. *Religious Violence and Abortion: The Gideon Project.* Gainesville: University Press of Florida.

Blasi, Anthony. 1989. *Early Christianity as a Social Movement.* New York: Peter Lang.

The Blue Book of the John Birch Society. 1959. Belmont, Mass.

Bonhoeffer, Dietrich. *Ethik.* Munich: Chr. Kaiser Verlag, 1966.

Boulding, Kenneth. 1964. *The Meaning of the Twentieth Century: The Great Transition.* New York: Harper and Row.

Brinkerhoff, Merlin B., and Eugen Pupri. 1988. "Religious Involvement and Spousal Abuse: The Canadian Case." Paper presented to the Society for the Scientific Study of Religion.

Bromley, David, and Anson Shupe. 1984. *New Christian Politics.* Macon, Ga.: Mercer University Press.

Bronowski, Jacob. 1973. *The Ascent of Man.* Boston: Little, Brown.

Brown, Judie. N.d. "The Human Life Amendment." N.p.

Brozan, Nadine. 1985. "Abortion Rights: New Tactics." *New York Times,* 6 May.

Bruce, Steve. 1988. *The Rise and Fall of the New Christian Right: Conservative Protestant Politics in America 1978–1988.* Oxford: Clarendon Press.

Burt, John. N.d. "Welcome to Our Father's House: A Place for New Beginnings." N.p.

Byrnes, Timothy A. 1991. *Catholic Bishops in American Politics.* Princeton, N.J.: Princeton University Press.

Cable, Sherry, Edward J. Walsh, and Rex H. Warland. 1988. "Differential Paths to Political Activism: Comparison of Four Mobilization Processes after the Three Mile Accident." *Social Forces* 66, no. 4 (June): 951–69.

Calhoun, C. 1983. *The Question of Class Struggle.* New York: Oxford University Press.

Callahan, Sidney, and Daniel Callahan, eds. 1984. *Abortion: Understanding Differences.* New York: Plenum Press.

Capitol Hill Christian News. December 1992. "(Stink) Bombs Away!" 7–8.

Caplan, Lincoln. 1989. "Pro-Life, Pro-Choice Antagonism: Political Provocations of Abortion." *Los Angeles Times,* 5 March.

Caron, Simone Marie. 1989. "Race, Class, and Reproduction: The Evolution of Reproductive Policy in the United States, 1800–1999." Ph.D. diss., Clark University.

Catholics for a Free Choice. 1986. *A Church Divided: Catholics' Attitudes about Family Planning, Abortion, and Teenage Sexuality.* Washington, D.C.

Christianity Today. 13 June 1986. "A New Political Group Will Oppose Abortion, Poverty, and Nuclear Arms," 36–37.

———. 2 October 1987. "Enlisting Blacks in the Battle against Abortion," 63–64.

Cimino, Richard P., ed. 1991. *Religion Watch* (North Bellmore, N.Y.) 7, no. 2 (December).

Clarke, Alan. 1987. "Collective Action against Abortion Represents a Display of, and Concern for, Cultural Values, Rather than an Expression of Status Discontent." *British Journal of Sociology* 38, no. 2: 235–53.

Clendinen, Dudley. 1985. "Abortion Clinic Bombings Have Caused Disruption for Many." *New York Times,* 23 January.

Coats, G. 1983. *Genesis with an Introduction to Narrative Literature.* Grand Rapids, Mich.: W. B. Eerdmans.

Cole, Stewart G. 1963. *The History of Fundamentalism*. Hamden, Conn.: Archon Books.

Collins, Randall. 1992 *Sociological Insight: An Introduction to Non-Obvious Sociology*. New York: Oxford University Press.

Commoner, Barry. 1974. "How Poverty Breeds Overpopulation (and Not the Other Way Around)." *Ramparts*, 21–25, 56–59.

Cook, Elizabeth Adell, Ted Jelen, and Clyde Wilcox. 1992. *Between Two Absolutes: Public Opinion and the Politics of Abortion*. Boulder, Colo.: Westview Press.

Condit, Celeste Mishelle. 1990. *Decoding Abortion Rhetoric: Communicating Social Change*. Urbana: University of Illinois Press.

Conway, Flo, and Jim Siegelman. 1982. *Holy Terror: The Fundamentalist War on America's Freedoms in Religion, Politics, and Our Private Lives*. New York: Delta Books.

Corbin, Beth. 1993. "Florida Physician Murdered by Clinic Terrorist." *National NOW Times,* April, 1, 3, 5.

Courry, Paul. 1991. "Abortion: Uprooting Operation Rescue." *Christianity and Crisis* 51, no. 7 (13 May): 160.

Cozart, William. "Cybernetics: Meta-Image of the Twentieth Century." *ie* (Chicago, Ecumenical Institute) 3, no. 2.

Crossfire. 4 January 1985. CNN.

_____. 24 May 1991. "The Price of Advice." CNN.

Crutcher, Mark. 1992. *Firestorm: A Guerrilla Strategy for a Pro-Life America*. Lewisville, Tex.: Life Dynamics.

Cuneo, Michael. 1989. *Catholics against the Church: Anti-Abortion Protest in Toronto, 1969–1985*. Toronto: University of Toronto Press.

Cuniberti, Betty, and Elizabeth Mehren. 1985. "Abortion Film Stirs Friend, Foe (*The Silent Scream*)." *Los Angeles Times,* 8 August.

Dallas Morning News. 17 March 1993. "Judge Fines Operation Rescue Despite Justices' Ruling."

D'Antonio, William V., and Steven Stack. 1980. "Religion, Ideal Family Size and Abortion: Extending Renzi's Hypothesis." *Journal for the Scientific Study of Religion,* December, 397–408.

Davall, Irene. 1991. "The Hand that Rocks the Cradle Can Also Rock the Boat. *On the Issues* 28 (Spring): 21.

De Berg, Betty A. 1991. *Ungodly Women: Gender and the First Wave of American Fundamentalism*. Minneapolis: Augsberg Fortress.

deParrie, Paul. 1993. "Situational Outrage." *Life Advocate* (Portland, Oregon). May, 43.

Diamond, Sara. 1989. *Spiritual Warfare: The Politics of the Christian Right*. Boston: South End Press.

Dionne, E. J., Jr. 1989a. "Abortion's Two Sides Crowd the Center." *New York Times,* 21 July.

_____. 1989b. "Poll Finds Ambivalence on Abortion Persists in U.S." *New York Times,* 3 August.

_____.1989c. "Two Sides in Abortion Debate Crowd the Center." *New York Times,* 13 August.

DiSalvo, Charles R. 1989. "What's Wrong with Operation Rescue?" *Commonweal* 116, no. 21 (1 December): 664–67.

Dixon, Amzi C., Louis Meyer, and Reuben A. Torrey, eds. 1910–15. 12 vols. *The Fundamentals: A Testimony to the Truth.* Chicago: Testimony Publishing.

Doe v. Bolton. 410 U.S. 1979 (1973).

Donenberg, Geri R., and L. W. Hoffman. 1988. "Gender Differences in Moral Development." *Sex Roles* 18: 701–17.

Donovan, Patricia. 1988. *When the Conventional Wisdom Is Wrong: A Reexamination of the Role of Abortion as an Issue in Federal Elections.* Washington, D.C.: Alan Guttmacher Institute.

Durham, Martin. 1986. "Class, Conservatism and the Anti-Abortion Movement: A Review Essay." *Berkeley Journal of Sociology* 31: 167–82.

Durkheim, Emile. 1893. *De la Division du Travail Social.* Paris: Alcan.

Ebaugh, H. F., and C. A. Haney. 1978. "Church Attendance and Attitudes toward Abortion: Differences in Liberal and Conservative Churches." *Journal for the Scientific Study of Religion,* 407–13.

Economist. 5 August 1989. "Abortion Right, Left," 29, 30.

Ehrlich, Paul, and Anne H. Ehrlich. 1968. *The Population Bomb.* New York: Ballantine Books.

Ellul, Jacques. 1965. *Propaganda.* New York: Knopf.

English, Deborah. 1981. "The War against Choice." *Mother Jones,* February.

Etzioni, Amitai. 1968. *The Active Society: A Theory of Societal and Political Processes.* New York: Free Press.

Face to Face with Connie Chung. 25 November 1989. "Fetal Tissue Research—Whose Right to Life?" Transcript from Journal Graphics, New York.

Falwell, Jerry. 1981. *Listen America!* New York: Bantam Books.

Farley, John E. 1987. *American Social Problems: An Institutional Analysis.* Englewood Cliffs, N.J.: Prentice-Hall.

Faux, Marian. 1988. *Roe v. Wade: The Untold Story of the Landmark Supreme Court Decision that Made Abortion Legal.* New York: New American Library.

_____. 1990. *Crusaders: Voices from the Abortion Front.* New York: Carol Publishing Group.

Fendrich, James. 1984. "Review of *Organized for Action: Commitment in Voluntary Associations,* by David H. Knoke and James R. Wood." *Social Forces* 63, no. 1: 305.

Ferguson, T., and J. Rogers. 1986. "The Myth of America's Turn to the Right." *Atlantic Monthly,* May, 43–53.

Festinger, Leon. 1957. *A Theory of Cognitive Dissonance.* Stanford, Calif.: Stanford University Press.

_____, Henry W. Rieken, and Stanley Schachter. 1956. *When Prophecy Fails.* Minneapolis: University of Minnesota Press.

Fichter, Joseph H. 1954. *Social Relations in the Urban Parish.* Chicago: University of Chicago Press.

Fields, Echo E. 1991. "Understanding Activist Fundamentalism: Capitalist Crisis and the 'Colonization of the Lifeworld.'" *Sociological Analysis* 52, no. 2 (Summer): 175–90.

Figueira-McDonough, Josefina. 1989. "Men and Women as Interest Groups in the Abortion Debate in the United States." *Women's Studies International Forum,* May, 539–50.

Foreman, Joseph Lapsley. 1992. *Shattering the Darkness: The Crisis of the Cross in the Church Today.* Montreat, N.C.: Cooling Spring Press.

48 Hours. 11 August 1993. "Choosing Sides." CBS News.

Fowler, Robert Booth. 1982. *A New Engagement: Evangelical Political Thought.* Grand Rapids, Mich.: Eerdmans.

Frame, Randy. 1985. "Violence against Abortion Clinics Escalates Despite the Opposition of Prolife Leaders." *Christianity Today,* 1 February, 44–45.

Franz, Wanda. N.d. [1992.] "ABC, CBS, & NBC Declare War on the Pro-Life Movement." Washington, D.C.: National Right to Life Committee.

Frenkel-Brunswick, Else. 1954. "Further Explorations by a Contributor to 'The Authoritarian Personality.'" In *Studies in the Scope and Method of "The Authoritarian Personality,"* edited by R. Christie and M. Jahoda. Glencoe, Ill.: Free Press.

Furstenberg, Frank F. 1976. *Unplanned Parenthood: The Consequences of Teenage Childbearing.* New York: Free Press.

Gallagher, Maggie. 1987. "Strange Bedfellows: The New Pro-Life Rebels." *National Review,* 27 February, 37–39.

Galotti, Kathleen M. 1975. *The Strategy of Social Protest.* Homewood, Ill.: Dorsey Press.

Gamson, William A. 1992. "The Social Psychology of Collective Action." In *Frontiers in Social Movement Theory,* edited by Aldon D. Morris and Carol McClung Mueller, 53–76. New Haven: Yale University Press.

Garfield, Jay L., and Patricia Hennessey, eds. 1984. *Abortion: Moral and Legal Perspectives.* Amherst: University of Massachusetts Press.

Gaspar, Louis. 1963. *The Fundamentalist Movement.* The Hague: Mouton.

Gillespie, Michael W. 1988. "Secular Trends in Abortion Attitudes." *Journal of Psychology,* July, 323–41.

Ginsburg, Faye. 1990. *Contested Lives: The Abortion Debate in an American Community.* Berkeley: University of California Press.

Gitlin, Todd. 1980. *The Whole World Is Watching.* Berkeley: University of California Press.

Goffman, Erving. 1981. *Forms of Talk*. Philadelphia: University of Pennsylvania Press.

Gold, Edwin M., Carl L. Erhart, Harold Jacobziner, and Frieda G. Nelson. 1965. "Therapeutic Abortions in New York State: A 20 Year Review." *American Journal of Public Health* 55 (July): 964–72.

Goldstein, Michael S. 1992. *The Health Movement: Fitness in America*. New York: Twayne Publishers.

Good Morning America. 25 July 1991. ABC News. Transcript from Journal Graphics, New York.

_____. 13 August 1991. ABC News. Transcript from Journal Graphics, New York.

Goodwin, Dave. 1992. "Abortion Protest Expected to Draw 8,000 to 10,000." *Pensacola News Journal*, 2 October.

Granberg, Donald. 1978. "Pro-Life or Reflection of Conservative Ideology? An Analysis of Opposition to Legalized Abortion." *Sociology and Social Research* 62 (April): 421–23.

_____. 1981. "The Abortion Activists." *Family Planning Perspectives* 13, no. 4: 158–61.

_____. 1982. "What Does It Mean to Be 'Pro-Life'?" *Christian Century*, 12 May, 562–66.

_____, and Beth Wellman Granberg. 1981. "Prolife Versus Prochoice: Another Look at the Abortion Controversy in the U.S." *Sociology and Social Research* 65, no. 4: 424–34.

Greenhouse, Linda. 1989. "Does the Right to Privacy Include the Right to Decide?" *New York Times*, 25 July.

Gunkel, Hermann. 1910. *Genesis*. 3d ed. Goettingen: Vandenhoeck and Ruprecht.

Gusfield, J. R. 1966. *Symbolic Crusade: Status Politics and the American Temperance Movement*. Urbana: University of Illinois Press.

Hall, Charles. 1993. "Social Networks and Availability Factors: Mobilizing Adherents for Social Movement Participation." Ph.D. diss., Purdue University.

Hall, Elaine J., and Myra Marx Ferree. 1986. "Race Differences in Abortion Attitudes." *Public Opinion Quarterly* 50, no. 2: 193–207.

Hall, Mimi. 1992a. "Abortion Opponents' New Weapon: Shock Ads." *USA Today*, 28 September.

_____. 1992b. "'Gag Rule' a Dilemma for Clinics." *USA Today*, 30 September.

Hall, Robert. 1965a. "Therapeutic Abortion, Sterilization, and Contraception." *American Journal of Obstetrics and Gynecology* 91 (15 February): 518–32.

_____. 1965b. "New York Abortion Law Survey." *American Journal of Obstetrics and Gynecology* 93 (15 December): 1182–83.

_____. 1967a. "Present Abortion Practices in Hospitals of New York State." *New York Medicine* 23 (March): 124–26.

_____. 1967b. "Abortion in American Hospitals." *American Journal of Public Health* 57 (November): 1933–36.

Harrell, David Edwin, Jr. 1975. *All Things Are Possible: The Healing and Charismatic Revivals in Modern America.* Bloomington: Indiana University Press.

Harrington, Michael. 1962. *The Other America: Poverty in the United States.* New York: Macmillan.

Herbers, John. 1986. "NOW Seeks to Curb Anti-Abortionists: Asks Court Injunction under Antitrust Statute to Limit Action against Clinics." *New York Times,* 11 June.

Hern, Warren M. 1989. "Abortion as Insurrection." *Humanist,* March/April, 18–20, 49.

Hill, Paul J. 1993. "Should We Defend Born and Unborn Children with Force?" Pensacola, Fla.: privately published, 14 pp.

Hilts, Philip J. 1991. "Official Tells of U.S. Plan to Steer Pregnant Women from Abortion." *New York Times,* 20 March.

Himmelstein, Jerome L. 1986. "The Social Basis of Antifeminism: Religious Networks and Culture." *Journal for the Scientific Study of Religion* 25, no. 1 (March): 1–15.

_____, and J. A. McRae 1984. "Social Conservatism, New Republicans, and the 1980 Election." *Public Opinion Quarterly* 48 (June): 592–605.

Holden, Constance. 1984. "A Pro-Life Population Delegation?" *Science,* June, 1321–22.

Houston, Paul. 1985. "White House Showcases Abortion Film." *Los Angeles Times,* 13 February.

Hunsberger, Bruce, and Bob Altemeyer. 1991. "Authoritarianism, Religious Fundamentalism, Quest and Prejudice." Paper presented at the annual meeting of the Society for the Scientific Study of Religion.

Hunter, James Davison. 1991. *Culture Wars: The Struggle to Define America.* New York: Basic Books.

Huser, Roger. 1942. *The Crime of Abortion in Canon Law.* Washington, D.C.: Catholic University Press.

Ireland, Patricia. 1989. "Racketeering Laws Side with Individual Rights." *National NOW Times,* May/June, 4.

Irwin, Theodore. 1970. "The New Abortion Laws: How Are They Working?" *Today's Health,* March, 21–22, 86.

Jaffe, Frederick S., Barbara L. Linheim, and Philip R. Lee. 1981. *Abortion Politics: Private Morality and Public Policy.* New York: McGraw-Hill Book Co.

Jenkins, Craig. 1983. "Resource Mobilization Theory and the Study of Social Movements." *Annual Review of Sociology* 9: 527–53.

Johnson, Stephen D., and Joseph B. Tamney. "Support for the Moral

Majority: A Test of a Model." *Journal for the Scientific Study of Religion* 23 (1984): 183–96.

Jorstad, Erling. 1970. *The Politics of Doomsday: Fundamentalism of the Far Right.* Nashville: Abingdon Press.

Kanter, Rosabeth. 1972. *Commitment and Community: Communes and Utopias in Sociological Perspective.* Cambridge, Mass.: Harvard University Press.

Kaplan, David A., and Bob Cohn. 1992. "The Hands-Off Court," *Newsweek,* 6 July, 32–36.

Kelly, Dean M. 1977. *Why Conservative Churches Are Growing.* New York: Harper and Row.

Kelly, James R. 1991. "Seeking a Sociologically Correct Name for Abortion Opponents." Paper presented at the annual meeting of the Society for the Scientific Study of Religion.

Keown, I. J. "Some Aspects of the Legal Regulation of Abortion in England from 1803 to 1982, with Particular Reference to the Influence of the Medical Profession on the Development of Law on the Practice of Abortion by the Medical Profession." Diss., University of Oxford, 1985.

Killian, Lewis M. 1972. "The Significance of Extremism in the Black Revolution." *Social Problems* 20 (Summer): 41–48.

Kinsey, Alfred C. 1954. *Sexual Behavior in the Human Female.* Philadelphia: Saunders.

Kirscht, John P., and Ronald C. Dillehay. 1967. *Dimensions of Authoritarianism: A Review of Research and Theory.* Lexington: University of Kentucky Press.

Kissling, Frances. 1991. "The Pope in Poor Company." *Conscience* 12, no. 6 (November/December): 21.

Kohlberg, Lawrence. *The Psychology of Moral Development.* New York: Harper and Row, 1983.

Kolata, Gina. 1990. "Under Pressures and Stigma, More Doctors Shun Abortion." *New York Times,* 8 January.

Komarovsky, Mirra. 1964. *Blue-Collar Marriage.* New York: Random House.

Koop, C. Everett, and Francis A. Schaeffer. 1983. *What Ever Happened to the Human Race?* Westchester, Ill.: Crossway Books.

Koppel Report. 19 December 1990. "Genetic Testing: A Mixed Blessing." ABC News. Transcript from Journal Graphics, New York.

Kriesberg, Louis, ed. 1985. *Research in Social Movements, Conflicts and Change.* Greenwich, Conn.: JAI Press.

Kurtz, Howard. 1989. "Operation Rescue: Agressively Antiabortion." *Washington Post,* 6 March.

Lacayo, Richard. 1992. "Abortion: The Future Is Already Here." *Time,* 4 May, 26–32.

Lader, Lawrence. 1966. *Abortion.* New York: Bobbs-Merrill.

LaHaye, Tim. 1980. *The Battle for the Mind.* Old Tappan, N.J.: Fleming H. Revell Co.

Lake, Randall A. 1986. "The Metaethical Framework of Anti-Abortion Rhetoric." *Signs,* Spring, 478–99.

Landis, Mark. 1987. *Joseph McCarthy: The Politics of Chaos.* Selinsgrove, Pa.: Susquehanna University Press.

Lawrence, Bruce B. 1989. *Defenders of God: The Fundamentalist Revolt against the Modern Age.* New York: Harper and Row.

Leahy, Peter J., and Allan Mazur. 1978. "A Comparison of Movements Opposed to Nuclear Power, Fluoridation, and Abortion." In *Research in Social Movements, Conflicts and Change,* vol. 1. Greenwich, Conn.: JAI Press.

Leahy, Peter J., David A. Snow, and Steven K. Worden. 1983. "The Anti-Abortion Movement and Symbolic Crusades: Reappraisal of a Popular Theory." *Alternative Lifestyles* 6, no. 1 (Fall): 27–47.

Levinson, D. J., and P. E. Huffman. 1955. "Traditional Family Ideology and Its Relationship to Personality." *Journal of Personality* 23: 251–73.

Lewin, Tamar. 1989. "Abortion Foes Lose Appeal over Rackets Law Damages." *New York Times,* 4 March: 1–9.

Lewis, Karen, Morton Rosenberg, and Allison I. Porter. 1981. *Abortion: Judicial and Legislative Control.* Washington, D.C.: Library of Congress.

Lewis, Neil A. 1989. "Florida High Court Nullifies a Law Restricting Abortions." *New York Times,* 6 October.

Liebman, Robert C., and Robert Wuthnow. 1983. *The New Christian Right.* New York: Aldine.

Lifton, Robert J. 1986. *The Nazi Doctors: Medical Killing and the Psychology of Genocide.* New York: Basic Books.

———, and Charles B. Strozier. 1990. "Waiting for Armageddon." *New York Times Book Review,* 12 August.

Lorentzen, Louise J. 1980. "Evangelical Life-Style Concerns Expressed in Political Action." *Sociological Analysis,* Summer, 144–54.

Luker, Kristin. 1984. *Abortion and the Politics of Motherhood.* Berkeley: University of California Press.

Luckmann, Thomas. 1967. *The Invisible Religion: The Problem of Religion in Modern Society.* New York: Macmillan.

McAdam, Doug. 1986. "Recruitment to High-Risk Activism: The Case of Freedom Summer." *American Journal of Sociology* 92: 64–90.

McCullough, Gary. 1993. "Griffin Is a Hero." *Life Advocate* (Portland, Oregon), May, 44.

Macdonald, Marci. 1985. "A Bitter *Silent Scream.*" *Maclean's,* 25 February, 58.

McIntosh, W. A., and Jon P. Alston. 1977. "Acceptance of Abortion among White Catholics and Protestants." *Journal for the Scientific Study of Religion* 16, no. 3 (September): 295–303.

McIntosh, W. A., L. T. Alston, and Jon P. Alston. 1979. "The Differential Impact of Religious Preference and Church Attendance on Attitudes toward Abortion." *Review of Religious Research*, 195–213.

Macon Telegraph. 14 March 1993. "Rescue America Founder: Abortion Protests Violent."

McRae v. Califano. 491 F.Supp. 630 (1980).

McRae v. Califano. 76 Civ. 1804, U.S. Dist. Court, Eastern Dist. of N.Y., Plaintiffs' First Amendment Brief.

Margolis, Michael, and Kevin Neary. 1980. "Pressure Politics Revisited: The Anti-Abortion Campaign." *Policy Studies Journal* B.5: 698–716.

Marty, Martin E. 1987. *Religion and Republic: The American Circumstance*. Boston: Beacon Press.

———, and R. Scott Appleby. 1992. *The Glory and the Power: The Fundamentalist Challenge to the Modern World*. Boston: Beacon Press.

———, eds. 1990. *Fundamentalisms Observed*. Chicago: University of Chicago Press.

Maxwell, Carol. 1991. "Where's the Land of Happy?: Individual Meanings in Pro-Life Direct Action." Paper presented at the Society for the Scientific Study of Religion.

———. 1992. "Denomination, Meaning, and Persistence: Difference in Individual Motivation to Obstruct Abortion Practice." Paper presented at the Society for the Scientific Study of Religion.

May, Lee. 1986. "Thousands of Abortion Foes Rally in Capital." *Los Angeles Times*, 23 January, 1–26.

Mietus, Norbert J. *The Therapeutic Abortion Act—A Statement in Opposition*. Sacramento: privately published, 1967.

Moen, Matthew C. "School Prayer and Politics of Life-Style Concern." *Social Science Quarterly* 65, no.4 (1984): 1065–71.

Mohr, James C. 1978. *Abortion in America: The Origins and Evolution of National Policy*. New York: Oxford University Press.

Morris, Aldon D., and Carol McClung Mueller, eds. 1992. *Frontiers in Social Movement Theory*, 133–55. New Haven, Conn.: Yale University Press.

Morris, Holly. 1989. "Reluctant Couple Converts to Activism." *Washington Post*, 2 February.

Moyers, Bill. 1991. "Abortion." *Bill Moyers Journal*. WNET-TV.

———, and Greg Pratt, eds. 1988. "On Earth as It Is in Heaven." In the television series *God and Politics*. PBS. Greg Pratt and Jan Falstad, producers.

Muller, Edward N., and R. Kenneth Godwin. 1984. "Democratic and Aggressive Political Participation: Estimation of a Nonrecursive Model." *Political Behavior* 6: 129–46.

Mumford, Lewis. 1961. *The City in History: Its Origins and Transformations, and Its Prospects*. New York: Harcourt, Brace and World.

Munby, D. L. 1963. *The Idea of a Secular Society and Its Significance for Christians.* Oxford: Oxford University Press.

Murdoch, William M. 1981. "Hungry Millions in a World that Could Feed All." *Los Angeles Times,* 18 October.

Nathanson, Bernard N. 1983. *The Abortion Papers: Inside the Abortion Mentality.* New York: Frederick Fell Publishers.

National Catholic Reporter. 14 November 1978. Review of *Are Catholics Ready?* by Maureen Fiedler and Dolly Pomerleau.

National NOW Times. 1991. "Nathanson to Pay for OR Involvement." March/April, 2.

Neitz, Mary Jo. 1981. "Family, State and God: Ideologies of the Right-to-Life Movement." *Sociological Analysis* 42: 265–76.

New Republic. 30 July 1990. "Notebook," 9.

New York Times. 26 January 1987. "Abortion Foes Ponder Setbacks."

_____. 16 August 1987. "Medical Use of Fetal Tissue Spurs New Abortion Debate."

_____. 12 December 1987. "Anti-Abortion Group Settles Oregon Lawsuit."

_____. 14 June 1992. "Thousands of Groups Press Movement against Abortion."

Nightline. 12 February 1985. "Abortion Controversy: *The Silent Scream.*" ABC News. Transcript from Journal Graphics, New York.

_____. 18 December 1985. "Abortion in a Pill." ABC News. Transcript from Journal Graphics, New York.

_____. 6 January 1988. "Fetal Transplants." ABC News. Transcript from Journal Graphics, New York.

_____. 31 March 1989. "The Abortion Pill." ABC News. Transcript from Journal Graphics, New York.

_____. 21 July 1989. "Anti-Abortionists Want Contraceptives Outlawed." ABC News. Transcript from Journal Graphics, New York.

_____. 6 August 1991. ABC News. Transcript from Journal Graphics, New York.

Noonan, J. T., Jr. 1967. "Abortion and the Catholic Church: A Summary History." *Natural Law Forum* 12: 85–131.

_____. 1968. "History of Abortion and the Church." *Theology Digest* 12: 251.

Nova. 26 June 1976. "The Genetic Chance." WGBH. Transcript from Journal Graphics, New York.

Oberschall, Anthony. 1978. "Loosely Structured Collective Conflict: A Theory and an Application." In *Research in Social Movements, Conflict and Change,* edited by Louis Kriesberg, vol. 1. Greenwich, Conn.: JAI Press.

Ogburn, William F. 1964. *On Culture and Social Change: Selected Papers.* Chicago: University of Chicago Press.

Olasky, Marvin N. 1986. "Opposing Abortion Clinics: A *New York Times* 1871 Crusade." *Journalism Quarterly* (3d quarter): 305–10.

Overstreet, H. A., and Bonaro Overstreet. 1964. *The Strange Tactics of Extremism.* New York: Norton.

Page, Ann L., and Donald A. Clelland. 1978. "The Kanawha County Textbook Controversy: A Study of the Politics of Life Style Concern." *Social Forces* 57, no. 1: 265–81.

Pensacola News Journal. 11 October 1989. "Anti-Racketeer Law Covers Abortion Foes."

———. 25 June 1992. "U.N. Report Says More Women Gaining Access to Birth Control."

———. 30 June 1992. "Abortion Ruling."

———. 27 October 1992. "Group Says Clinics for Abortions Were Ruse."

Perry, William G., Jr. 1970. *Forms of Intellectual and Ethical Development in the College Years: A Scheme.* New York: Holt, Rinehart and Winston.

Petchetsky, Rosalind P. 1984. *Abortion and Woman's Choice: The State, Sexuality, and Reproductive Freedom.* New York: Longman.

Photiadis, J., and A. Johnson. 1963. "Orthodoxy, Church Participation, and Authoritarianism." *American Journal of Sociology* 69: 244–48.

Piaget, Jean. 1967. *Six Psychological Studies.* New York: Random House.

Planned Parenthood Federation of America. 1989. *Public Affairs Action Letter* 5, no. 19 (12 May): 4.

———. 1991. *Public Affairs Action Letter* 7, no. 16 (19 April): 4.

———. 1992a. *Public Affairs Action Letter* 8, no. 4 (31 January): 3.

———. 1992b. *Public Affairs Action Letter* 8, no. 5 (7 February): 4.

———. 1992c. *Public Affairs Action Letter* 8, no. 6 (14 February): 4.

———. 1992d. *Public Affairs Action Letter* 8, no. 8 (28 February): 4.

———. 1992e. *Public Affairs Action Letter* 8, no. 15 (17 April): 3–4.

———. 1992f. *Public Affairs Action Letter* 8, no. 21 (5 June): 6.

———. 1992g. *Public Affairs Action Letter* 8, no. 22 (12 June): 4.

———. 1992h. *Public Affairs Action Letter* 8, no. 26 (10 July): 3–4.

———. 1992i. *Public Affairs Action Letter* 8, no. 28 (24 July): 4.

———. 1992j. *Public Affairs Action Letter* 8, no. 34 (11 September): 4.

Pollock, C. B., and B. F. Steele. 1968. "A Psychiatric Study of Parents Who Abuse Infants and Small Children." In *The Battered Child,* edited by R. E. Helfer and C. H. Kemp. Chicago: University of Chicago Press.

Population and Development Review. 1989. "The U.S. Surgeon General on the Health Effects of Abortion." March 172–75.

Pratt, Lawrence D. N.d. [1990]. Letter to "Dear Friend of the Family." St. Louis: Committee to Protect the Family Foundation.

Prescott, James W. 1989. "The Abortion of *The Silent Scream.*" In *Abortion Rights and Fetal "Personhood,"* edited by Edd Doerr and James W. Prescott. Long Beach, Calif.: Centerline Press.

Price, Joyce. 1992. "Clinton Victory Is Huge Setback for Abortion Foes." *Washington Times,* 5 November.

Primetime Live. 31 October 1991. "Lying in Wait." ABC News. Transcript from Journal Graphics, New York, pp. 3–8.

Quadeer, Mohammed. 1975. "Why Family Planning Is Failing." *Social Policy* 6, no. 3 (November–December): 20–23.

Rauschenbusch, Walter. 1918. *A Theology for the Social Gospel.* New York: Macmillan.

Reagan, Ronald. 1983. "Abortion and the Conscience of the Nation." *Human Life Review,* Spring.

Redekop, John H. 1968. *The American Far Right.* Grand Rapids: William B. Eerdman's.

Roberts, Keith A. 1986. "Sociology in the General Education Curriculum: A Cognitive Structuralist Perspective." *Teaching Sociology* 14 (October): 207–16.

Roe v. Wade, 410 U.S. 113 (1973).

Rosenberg, Ellen M. 1989. "Serving Jesus in the South: Southern Baptist Women Under Assault from the New Right." *Women in the South: An Anthropological Perspective.* Macon, Ga.: University of Georgia Press.

Ryan, Charlotte. 1991. *Prime Time Activism.* Boston: South End Press.

Salhoz, Eloise. 1992. "Abortion Angst." *Newsweek,* 13 July, 16–19.

Sarvis, Betty, and Hyman Rodman. 1974. *The Abortion Controversy.* New York: Columbia University Press.

Scheidler, Joseph M. 1985. *Closed: 99 Ways to Stop Abortion.* Westchester, Ill.: Crossway Books.

Schwartz, Amy. 1985. "Bitter Pill." *New Republic,* 18 February, 10–12.

Scott, Jacqueline. 1989. "Conflicting Beliefs about Abortion: Legal Approval and Moral Doubts." *Social Psychology Quarterly* 52, no. 4: 319–26.

Shils, E. A. 1954. "Authoritarianism Right and Left." In *Studies in the Scope and Method of "The Authoritarian Personality,"* edited by R. Christie and M. Jahoda. Glencoe, Ill.: Free Press.

Showalter, Elaine. 1990. *Gender and Culture at the Fin de Siècle.* New York: Viking Penguin.

Shupe, Anson, and John Heinerman. 1985. "Mormonism and the New Christian Right: An Emerging Coalition?" *Review of Religious Research* 27, no. 2: 146–57.

60 Minutes. 14 August 1977. "Point-Counterpoint." CBS News. Transcript from Journal Graphics, New York.

———. 4 October 1981. "Mr. Right-to-Life." CBS News. Transcript from Journal Graphics, New York.

Smidt, Corwin E. 1989. "'Praise the Lord' Politics: A Comparative Analysis of the Social Characteristics and Political Views of American Evangelical and Charismatic Christians." *Sociological Analysis* 50, no. 1: 53–72.

Smith, Lynn. 1989. "Four Voice Their Operation Rescue Stories." *Los Angeles Times-Mirror,* 23 March.

_____, and Carol McGraw. 1989. "Long Beach Lets Abortion Protest Wither." *Los Angeles Times,* 25 March.

Snow, David A., and Robert D. Benford. 1988. "Ideology, Frame Resonance, and Participant Mobilization." In *From Structure to Action: Comparing Social Movement Research across Cultures,* edited by Bert Klandermans, Hanspeter Kriesi, and Sydney Tarrow. International Social Movement Research, vol. 1. Greenwich, Conn.: JAI Press.

_____. 1992. "Master Frames and Cycles of Protest." In *Frontiers in Social Movement Theory,* edited by Aldon D. Morris and Carol McClung Mueller, 133–55. New Haven, Conn.: Yale University Press.

Snow, David A., E. Burke Rochford, Jr., Steven K. Worden, and Robert D. Benford. 1986. "Frame Alignment Processes, Micromobilization, and Movement Participation." *American Sociological Review* 51 (August): 464–68.

Snow, David A., Louis A. Zurcher, Jr., and Sheldon Ekland-Olson. 1980. "Social Networks and Social Movements." *American Sociological Review* 45: 787–801.

Snowball, David. 1991. *Continuity and Change in the Rhetoric of the Moral Majority.* New York: Praeger.

Specter, Michael. 1990. "Fetal-Tissue Research Ban Formally Extended." *Washington Post,* 3 November.

Spitzer, Robert J. 1987. *The Right to Life Movement and Third Party Politics.* Westport, Conn.: Greenwood Press.

Staggenborg, Susan. 1988. "The Consequences of Professionalization and Formalization in the Pro-Choice Movement." *American Sociological Review* 53, no. 4: 585–606.

Steinfels, Peter. 1988. "Dissecting Fundamentalism, the Principles and the Name." *New York Times,* 20 November.

_____. 1990. "New Voice, Same Words on Abortion." *New York Times,* 20 November.

Steinhoff, Patricia G., and Milton Diamond. 1977. *Abortion Politics: The Hawaii Experience.* Honolulu: University Press of Hawaii.

Stets, Jan E. 1991. "Attitudes about Abortion and Varying Attitude Structures." Paper presented at the annual meeting of the American Sociological Association.

Suall, Irwin. 1962. *The American Ultras: The Extreme Right and the Military-Industrial Complex.* New York: League for Industrial Democracy.

Suh, Mary, and Lydia Denworth. 1989. "The Gathering Storm: Operation Rescue." *Ms.,* April, 92–93.

Tapp, Robert P. 1973. *Religion among the Unitarian-Universalists: Converts in the Father's House.* New York: Seminar Press.

Terry, Randall. 1988. *Operation Rescue.* Springdale, Pa.: Whitaker House.

Thomas, Aquinas. 1962. *Summa Theologica.* Englewood Cliffs, N.J.: Prentice-Hall.

Thomas, Cal. 1988. "Civil Disobedience against Abortion May Go National." *Los Angeles Times-Mirror*, 29 August.

Tierney, John. 1986. "Fanisi's Choice." *Science*, January/February, 26–42.

Time. 4 May 1992. "The Shouting of the Lambs," 30.

Toner, Robin. 1986. "Foes of Abortion Exhorted by Reagan at Capital Rally." *New York Times*, 23 January.

Toronto, Joan C. 1987. "Moral Orientations: Both Justic and Care." *Signs* 12: 644–63.

Traina, Frank J. 1975. "Diocesan Mobilization against Abortion Law Reform." Diss., Cornell University.

Tumulty, Karen. 1989. "Words—Potent Weapon in Fight over Abortion." *Los Angeles Times*, 23 March.

_____, and Lynn Smith. 1989. "Operation Rescue: Soldier in a 'Holy War' on Abortion." *Los Angeles Times-Mirror*, 17 March.

Turner, Ralph H., and Lewis M. Killian. *Collective Behavior*. Englewood Cliffs, N.J.: Prentice-Hall, 1987.

Uehling, Mark D. 1986. "Clinics of Deception: Pro-lifers Set Up Shop." *Newsweek*, 1 September, 20.

Useem, Michael. 1975. *Protest Movements in America*. Indianapolis: Bobbs-Merrill.

Vanderford, Marsha L. 1989. "Vilification and Social Movements: A Case Study of Prolife and Prochoice Movements." *Quarterly Journal of Speech*, May, 166–82.

van Til, Cornelius. 1967a. *The Defense of the Faith*. Philadelphia: Presbyterian and Reformed Publishing Co.

_____. 1967b. *A Christian Theory of Knowledge*. Philadelphia: Presbyterian and Reformed Publishing Co.

_____. 1967c. *The New Hermeneutic*. Nutley, N.J.: Presbyterian and Reformed Publishing Co.

Van Winden, Lori. 1988. *The Case against Abortion: A Logical Argument for Life*. Liguori, Mo.: Liguori Publications.

Vinzant, Carol. 1993. "Fetus Frenzy." *Spy*, May, 58–65.

Volpe, E. Peter. 1984. *The Patient in the Womb*. Macon, Ga.: Mercer University Press.

von Rad, G. 1972. *Genesis: A Commentary*. Philadelphia: Westminster Press.

Wallace, Anthony F. C. 1956. "Revitalization Movements." *American Anthropologist* 58.

Wallis, Roy. "A Critique of the Theory of Moral Crusades as Status Defense. *Scottish Journal of Sociology* 1, no. 2: 195–203.

Washington Post. 20 January 1984. "Abortion Wars."

_____. 9 August 1990. "Antiabortion Activists to Boycott Companies."

Weiser, Benjamin. 1985. "Antiabortion Underground Operated in D.C. Hospital." *Washington Post*, 30 March.

The West. 28 April 1991. "Fetal Scan." Transcript from Journal Graphics, New York.

Westcoff, C. F., C. E. Moore, and N. B. Ryder. 1969. "The Structure of Attitudes toward Abortion." *Millbank Memorial Fund Quarterly* 47, no. 11.

Whitney, Catherine. 1991. *Whose Life?* New York: William Morrow and Company.

Wickenden, Dorothy. 1990. "Drug of Choice." *New Republic,* 16 November, 24–27.

Wiener, Norbert. 1950. *The Human Use of Human Beings: Cybernetics and Society.* Boston: Houghton Mifflin.

Wilcox, Mary. 1979. *Developmental Journey: A Guide to the Development of Logical and Moral Reasoning and Social Perspective.* Nashville: Abingdon.

Wilson, John. 1983. "Corporatism and the Professionalization of Reform." Journal of Political and Military Sociology 11: 53–68.

Wilson, Michele, and John Lynxwiler. 1988. "Abortion Clinic Violence as Terrorism." *Terrorism* 11, no. 4: 263–73.

Williams, Roger M. 1979. "The Power of Fetal Politics. *Saturday Review* 6 (9 June): 12–15.

Wong, Pamela Pearson. 1987. "Attracting Clients and Controversy." *Christianity Today,* 18 September, 32–33.

Wood, M., and M. Hughes. 1984. "The Moral Basis of Moral Reform: Status Discontent vs. Culture and Socialization as Explanations of Anti-Pornography Social Movement Adherence." *American Sociological Review* 44: 86–99.

Woodrum, Eric, and Beth L. Davison. 1992. "Reexamination of Religious Influences on Abortion Attitudes." *Review of Religious Research* 33, no. 2: 229–43.

World News Tonight. 6 August 1991. ABC News. Transcript from Journal Graphics, New York.

_____. 7 August 1991. ABC News. Transcript from Journal Graphics, New York.

Zald, Mayer N. 1980. "Issues in the Theory of Social Movements." *Perspectives in Social Theory* 1, 61–72.

_____, and Roberta Ash. 1966. "Social Movement Organizations: Growth, Decay, and Change." *Social Forces* 44: 327–40.

_____, and John D. McCarthy, eds. *Social Movements in an Organizational Context.* New Brunswick, N.J.: Transaction Books, 1987.

Zelnick, M., and J. F. Kantner. 1977. "Sexual and Contraceptive Experience of Young Unmarried Women in the United States, 1976 and 1971." *Family Planning Perspectives* 9, no. 55.

Index

The Author

Dallas A. Blanchard is associate professor and chair of the Department of Sociology and Anthropology at the University of West Florida, Pensacola. He holds an A.B. from Birmingham-Southern College, an M.Div. from Vanderbilt University, and a Ph.D. in the sociology of religion and social ethics from Boston University, and he is coauthor with Terry J. Prewitt of *Religious Violence and Abortion: The Gideon Project* (1993). He is also a minister in the Alabama-West Florida Conference of the United Methodist Church.